JOCELYN HERBERT

A Theatre Workbook edited by Cathy Courtney

JOCELYN HERBERT

A Theatre Workbook edited by Cathy Courtney

ART BOOKS INTERNATIONAL · LONDON

First published in 1993 by Art Books International

1 Stewart's Court
220 Stewart's Road
London SW8 4UD

© *Jocelyn Herbert & Cathy Courtney*

ISBN 1-874044-05-8

British Cataloguing-in-Publication Data.
Catalogue record for this book is available from the
British Library.

Design, art edit and production by Eitetsu Nozawa
Design Assistant Michael Hopkins

Printing and binding by Toppan Printing, *Singapore.*

Photo: John Haynes

To George Devine

J.H.

This book would not have been possible without the enlightened sponsorship of The David Cohen Family Charitable Trust, The Elephant Trust, The Linbury Trust and The Rayne Foundation, whose help rescued the publication at the eleventh hour.

Even with the backing of our sponsors, we would not have been able to include any production photographs were it not for the generosity of the photographers whose work appears in the book, all of whom allowed us to use their pictures without payment. Every effort has been made to contact the owners of copyright material reproduced in this volume. Apologies are offered in advance for any unauthorised usage.

I would also like to thank Jocelyn's colleagues, who have devoted thought and time to the book and shown great kindness and patience towards me.

The Workbook's designer, Eitetsu Nozawa, has remained unflaggingly loyal throughout the many changes which have attended the project's development and his support has been crucial in bringing it to fruition. Stanley Kekwick and Shaunagh Heneage of Art Books International, our publishers, were willing to back the book when few others would and I am indebted to them. I would also like to thank Jane Brodie, Hugh and Margaret Casson, Alison Chitty, John Christie, Jessica Courtney, Carlene Crowe, Bob Crowley, Richard Eyre, Julia Farrer, Margaret Fournier, Penelope Gilliatt, Charlotte Goodfield, David Gothard, Michael Hopkins, Caradoc King, Ronald King, Linda Shaughnessy, Peter Townsend and Ian Tyson for their help, both practical and emotional, at various stages along the way. Naturally, my deepest thanks are due to the person who has contributed most to the book, Jocelyn Herbert.

Cathy Courtney

Preface

This book is a record of the work of Jocelyn Herbert. The main body of the text has been edited from conversations between Jocelyn and myself as we looked through the over 4,000 drawings that form her archive. The first section documents Jocelyn's career with the English Stage Company, mainly at The Royal Court; the second, productions for The National Theatre; and the third brings together her designs for theatres outside these categories. There then follows a section on opera. The almost sixty year span of Jocelyn's working life covers one of the richest periods of British theatre history and includes the first performances of many of the plays which have subsequently come to be regarded as modern classics. For reasons of space it has been impossible to illustrate every production on which Jocelyn has collaborated but the cast lists at the back include them all in chronological order.

There are countless books on actors and directors but virtually none on the contribution of the designer, whose role is little understood and almost never discussed by audiences and critics. I can think of no other book which looks in depth at the work of a contemporary British stage designer. The relative neglect of such a vital creative strand in our theatre can partly be explained by the paradox that many of our most distinguished practitioners aim to be as little noticed as possible, believing it a measure of success in serving the playwright if the setting goes unremarked and appears so integrated with the style of the writing and performing as to be inseparable from them.

This Workbook tries to re-create a little of the chemistry that at its best flows between director, designer and writer throughout the process of bringing a play to the stage, and to show how deeply the design may influence the production values as a whole. It has been a characteristic of Jocelyn's career that she has formed long working relationships with several key directors and writers, many of whom first met at George Devine's Royal Court Theatre, and, where applicable, I have included their comments alongside Jocelyn's own in the discussion of how the problems of each play were resolved. Longer contributions from colleagues appear in the last section of the book. Where there has been a divergence of opinion I have included both views intentionally.

This volume has been a long time in the making and, sadly, during its gestation we have lost several of the contributors. Peggy Ashcroft, Samuel Beckett, John Dexter, Ronald Eyre, Suria Magito and Tony Richardson died before its publication and, in addition to its other functions, the book now forms an archive for their words.

✳ ✳ ✳ ✳ ✳

The daughter of A.P. Herbert, Jocelyn was born in 1917 and grew up in a household where painters, writers and theatre people were frequent visitors. She studied painting with André Lhote in Paris and trained in theatre design at the Slade School of Art before joining The London Theatre Studio (LTS) in 1936. Directors Michel Saint-Denis and George Devine and the famous Motley design team – Margaret Harris, Sophie Harris and Elizabeth Montgomery – were her teachers, and their productions outside the school were also a formative influence.

Jocelyn's training at the LTS was cut short by the war. In 1938 she married Anthony Lousada, and by 1945 she had four children, Sandra (many of whose photographs appear in this book), Jenny (who was later to assist her on several productions, chiefly with making masks) and twins, Julian and

Olivia. She chose to put her career aside in order to bring up her family and her working life has always been combined with strong personal ties.

Jocelyn joined George Devine's English Stage Company (ESC) at The Royal Court in 1956 and designed her first production, Ionesco's *The Chairs*, the following year. The Court became the home for a generation of writers and Jocelyn was at the heart of it, working on new material by John Arden, Arnold Wesker, John Osborne, Samuel Beckett and David Storey. It was here that she first collaborated with Lindsay Anderson, John Dexter and Tony Richardson, also at the outset of their careers, and the text of this book recaptures some of the atmosphere in which their working relationships were born. Eventually Jocelyn's marriage to Anthony Lousada was dissolved and she and George Devine lived together, uniting work and home life, until the latter's death in 1966.

The values which Jocelyn absorbed and contributed to at The Court are ones she carries with her wherever she works. This book charts not only her remarkable consistency and strength but also the landmarks in design for which she was responsible – for example the use of the naked stage with back wall and lighting-rig in full view (*The Kitchen*, 1959) and the large-scale use of metal at Stratford-on-Avon (*Richard III*, 1961) – which audiences now take for granted. Over fifty years after she became a student at the LTS, Jocelyn is as ready to set about staging *Timon of Athens* in the tiny studio of Leicester's Haymarket Theatre with a cast of seven actors and a design budget of £420.00 as she is to introduce a revolutionary simplicity to the vast space of New York's Metropolitan Opera. Still preferring to work with new material, she was the natural designer for the ENO's 1986 world première of Harrison Birtwistle's opera *The Mask of Orpheus*, and her continuing collaboration with Tony Harrison is proving to be one of the richest in her career, with the 1992 production of *Square Rounds* (on which her granddaughter, the designer Polly Richards, worked as her assistant) perhaps illustrating better than any other the interdependency of writer/director and designer.

* * * * *

I first met Jocelyn in 1979 when she was sixty two. She had her arm in a sling following an accident roller-skating in Central Park with her son. Later, I found out that the skates were a first night present from the design department at The Metropolitan Opera where she had been designing Mozart's *Die Entführung aus dem Serail*. The story contains the elements which define her life; love of family, commitment to work of the highest calibre, a willingness to take risks, and the fellow-feeling she inspires in her workmates. Her influence is as strong offstage as on, demonstrated in her steadfast loyalties and values, her long-term role on the Council of The Royal Court and in her continuing administration of The George Devine Award. If many distinguished colleagues and friends have been willing to give time and thought to this book it is a measure of the respect and affection with which she is held in the world of British theatre. Jocelyn Herbert is a deeply modest person and one of our few disagreements has been over the inclusion of the tributes paid to her by her colleagues which appear at various points in the book. I had no doubt that they should stay.

Cathy Courtney

Contents

Introduction

chest 35.

waist 29.

hips 37.

out leg 40½.

in " 29

7½ 20.30½.

collar 14½

Whitehead

Introduction

I was trained at the London Theatre Studio run by Michel Saint-Denis and George Devine. The design course was taught by a group of distinguished designers – Sophie Harris, Margaret Harris and Elizabeth Montgomery, who worked together under the name of Motley. Richard Southern taught the technical aspects of stage scenery and its development through the ages, as well as technical drawings etc. All students, whether acting, directing or designing, attended lectures on the history of the theatre, how to approach a text, the varying demands made by texts of different periods and from other countries and how to find a style that would be good for the text but also help to communicate it to a contemporary audience. Apart from improvisation and mask work, I think we mostly worked on classical plays. Actors had to help make costumes and scenery for the school shows and designers had to act, stage manage and do lighting etc. Everyone went to lighting lectures. Michel's attitude to the theatre was a way of life, a search for perfection in which everyone's talents contributed. He taught that people who worked in the theatre should know how to value the work of each person involved and what it entailed, whatever their department. His theatre had nothing to do with the star system and everything to do with working as a company where everyone was a star.

I finished training in 1938, but the war, getting married and having four children put an end to designing until 1956, when George Devine became Artistic Director of The Royal Court Theatre and asked me to join his company as a scene painter. There was very little fringe theatre in those days and West End productions were weighed down with heavily naturalistic and decorative scenery and were mostly revivals of classics or drawing room type comedies. George wanted to have a writers' theatre where the text and the actors were more important than the director and designer. He wanted to clear the stage and let in the light and air and give a home to writers who were concerned with the times we lived in and the problems that beset us all. This is, of course, well known and his ten years at The Royal Court gave a new life blood to the British theatre. There was a particular excitement in giving birth to new plays, and when we came to work on a classic we realised it could be approached with the same excitement; the freedom of staging that we had discovered was possible with the contemporary plays was a great influence on our interpretation of the old ones. It was during this time that I began to work with the group of directors who also started their careers at The Royal Court, especially Tony Richardson, Lindsay Anderson, John Dexter and Bill Gaskill, who remained friends and colleagues ever since.

The Royal Court is a small theatre, but it has a beautifully proportioned stage and the limited wing space is compensated by a good grid and under-stage traps. These limitations naturally influence your design when you work there, but in my experience physical limitations and budget restrictions can, sometimes, result in a more interesting or imaginative production stylistically than you might have come up with without them.

The first ten years at The Royal Court when George Devine was Artistic Director was a very special time for everyone who worked there. George created a place where people could grow. Everyone fed off him, off his knowledge and experience, his humour and his humanity and the way he welcomed and nurtured talent wherever he found it. He loved the theatre in all its aspects and he believed the theatre could and should take its place among the other arts, and it was that belief and the atmosphere it engendered that made The Court such an inspiring place to work in. George Devine was a great man, not only of the theatre but as a human being, and his rare spirit is sadly missed today.

Finally, for me, there seems no *right way* to design a play, only, perhaps, a *right approach*. One of respecting the text, past or present, and not using it as a peg to advertise your skills, whatever they may be, nor to work out your psychological hang-ups with some fashionable gimmick.

Jocelyn Herbert

Costume drawing for The Fair, *first school show at the LTS.*

Costume drawings for The Disasters of War, *based on Goya. Second year show at the LTS.*

The Royal Court Theatre & The English Stage Company

The Stage and Auditorium of The Royal Court Theatre.
Photos: John Haynes

The Good Woman of Setzuan

Bertolt Brecht, *Director:* George Devine, *Designer:* Teo Otto
31 October 1956, *The Royal Court Theatre (first British performance).*

Jocelyn Herbert supervised the building of the set according to Teo Otto's instructions. Peggy Ashcroft played the title role of the kind-hearted prostitute Shen Te, a part which required her to disguise herself as a ruthless and greedy young man, Shui Ta. Jocelyn persuaded her to wear a mask for the first time in her career, to help her move more easily between the male and female roles.

JH: The production was designed by Teo Otto of the Berliner Ensemble, but he didn't come over to England so we had to interpret his instructions. The breakdown of props and costumes was vital and, as we had just seen the Berliner Ensemble in London, it was a challenge to produce something of that quality. It was a lovely set, very simple, made with just large brick-red bamboo poles and matting screens which moved up and down between the poles to change the scene. Peggy Ashcroft had never been in anything like *The Good Woman of Setzuan* before. She was very against wearing a mask to begin with, but in the end it liberated her. It was made of leather so it was light and supple.

Peggy Ashcroft: I always see the character I am going to play, and I visualise it quite outside myself. Finally it comes back to me that I've only got my own face, and I suffer to a certain extent a terrible feeling of disillusion – that I'm not as transformed as I would like to be. I said to George Devine that I would like to feel I could move from one sex to the other using just the costume, but he suggested I might find a mask exciting and helpful. I remember the horrible process of having it made – my face was covered with plaster. The mask was very light and it thrilled me to see its effect on me. It was very, very exciting. I think my idea of a mask had been something much less plastic, much harder and more confining, but this little affair was the reverse of that.

Peggy Ashcroft wearing the mask from The Good Woman of Setzuan *in a reconstruction of the character in 1988: "The mask is marvellously flexible. I've still got it and it's been worn by all my grandchildren over the years. Even the little moustache has stayed."*
Photo: Sandra Lousada

The Chairs

Eugene Ionesco (translated by Donald Watson), *Director:* Tony Richardson
14 May 1957, The Royal Court Theatre (first production in Britain).

The Chairs had been performed in Paris in 1952, but Ionesco's work was very little known in England. The stage directions asked for a single set with circular walls, two windows, a monumental double door and a series of further single doors (some not visible to the audience). Crucial to the atmosphere of the production was the sense that the set was surrounded by water.

JH: *The Chairs* was my first set at The Royal Court and I took a long time to get it right. I just kept reading and reading the play and listening to Tony Richardson. He had lots of ideas, but I never could make any of them work; I hadn't yet learnt that I didn't have to do exactly what a director asked for. Eventually I did one very rough sketch and thought it had the right feel to it. I put it among the other sketches I'd done and asked Tony to choose and, to my relief, he picked out the one I thought would work; it was of a place which had no architectural reality.

I wanted to build the walls using rope fixed to curved bars at the top and bottom. A rope hung on both sides of each of the doors and windows and the area above them was a mixture of painted canvas panels and empty spaces through which the audience could see the cyc[1]. Each canvas panel was painted individually so as to give the feeling of water. The Ionesco was playing in a double bill with *The Apollo de Bellac*[2] for which I had to paint an extremely complicated false perspective set that I found very difficult to do. It was very strange having the huge *Apollo* set in the workshop beside the bits of rope with panels on them that I'd designed for *The Chairs*. I'd got the rope stretched but all the canvas had to be painted and it looked unbelievable, like a load of old junk.

During the set-up I was in a panic that it was not going to work. The hanging parts were wobbling about and the stage hands were roaring with laughter. By five o'clock in the morning we'd got all the hanging ropes with their doors and panels on the circular bar and the central door was in place. It looked like nothing on earth, and I was in a state of complete terror. I went to sit in the Circle as the cyc went up and, gradually, the whole thing took shape and suddenly I felt quite calm and knew it would be all right. George Devine appeared at the moment when I was just about to burst into tears with relief.

In the play all the doors have to open and close as if a crowd of invisible people are coming onto the stage and the old couple go in and out bringing in more chairs. At the dress rehearsal we still hadn't decided how to make the doors work together and I suggested we ask all the stage hands to do it. It worked beautifully and they loved doing it. I was sitting in the Circle, and I remember at the end a voice beside me suddenly said, "That's the sort of theatre we've been waiting for." It was Oscar Lewenstein, who had helped found the ESC and was on The Court's council.

The stage hands came up after the dress rehearsal and said it wasn't so bad a set after all. I've felt all my life that if the people backstage liked what I'd done it was more important to me than anything else because their reaction is completely spontaneous and not intellectual in any way. Technically, *The Chairs* could have been better achieved if I hadn't had to do it all myself in about five minutes. For instance, we had very little time to make the big golden door and I tried to do the translucences using gold paper and glazes, but it didn't really work. There are so many other materials now that you can use, in terms of metal gauzes, which would have been more effective and less glary. It could have been better, but it worked quite well.

I suppose I gained a bit of confidence by designing *The Chairs*, and began to believe that the way I was thinking about decor might have something in it. I felt I had started again, with a vision of my own. It helped me to go on trying to work in a more abstract way, to discover a form of poetic realism.

Top *The sketch chosen by Tony Richardson as the basis for* The Chairs *set.*

Left *The set beginning to fill up with chairs as the play proceeds.*

Tony Richardson: The best of the older generation had sets and just put light on them, but didn't conceive of them in terms of light and scenery working together. I think, because of Jocelyn's involvement in the world of painting and drawing, she was more receptive to the concept of light on scenery. Her set for *The Chairs* was able to change and had immense variations. I wasn't aware of her being worried.

1 *Cyclorama: white backcloth, usually curved.*
2 *Jean Giraudoux. Directed by Tony Richardson, designed by Carl Toms.*

Left *Costume drawing for the Old Woman, played by the twenty nine year old Joan Plowright.*

Right *Costume drawing for the Old Man (George Devine).*

George Devine   The Old Man

"The Chair"

Purgatory

W.B. Yeats, *Director:* John Dexter

22 July 1957, produced by the English Stage Company for the Devon Festival.

Yeats calls for a ruined house and a bare tree in the background.

JH: I didn't know John Dexter all that well at this time. He insisted on having an old tree as a kind of altar, whereas I just wanted to have the burnt-out shell of the house with steps down and said that was the altar. Years and years later he admitted to me that the tree didn't work. The fact is that, if you have a director who really feels he needs something, you finally have to give it to him; you can't not, even though you think it's wrong and it doesn't fit with your attitude to the play.

John Dexter: The play called for a window and a door, and that's what we did. It was an absolutely simple relationship. Jocelyn came up with a very simple structure which worked for me. I'd got two people on stage for twenty minutes and I needed the tree as a separate place from the centre where people could sit down.

The Sport of My Mad Mother

Ann Jellicoe: *Directors: George Devine & Ann Jellicoe*
25 February 1958, The Royal Court Theatre (world première).

The play takes place down a back street, "a protected corner". As it begins one of the characters, Steve, arranges a drum, motor horn, triangle and cymbals on the side of the stage.

JH: This was the first really experimental play we did at The Court – with a more or less abstract set – creating a space where the text and the action could function without being restricted by the naturalism of a specific setting. It was also the first time that we saw Ann Jellicoe's very personal magic touch with actors and the vitality and imagination she brought to directing.

Top and above *Production photographs for* The Sport of My Mad Mother.
Photos: Roger Mayne

Right *Costume drawing for Greta (Wendy Craig).*

25

Costume drawings for The Sport of My Mad Mother.

Endgame

Samuel Beckett, *Directors:* Donald McWhinnie & George Devine
28 October 1958, The Royal Court Theatre (first English language production).

The stage directions ask for a bare interior; two small high windows back left and right; a door;
a picture; two ashbins, each covered with an old sheet; an armchair covered with an old sheet.

JH: The first ever *Endgame* production was when the French company came over in 1957. They couldn't get a theatre in Paris and George Devine said they could do it at The Court. *Fin de Partie* was directed by Roger Blin, with a set by Jacques Noel. I was in charge of the decor department so I painted the scenery and was responsible for getting the set ready. I'd never seen a Beckett play before. I remember reading it and saying to George, "I don't know how anyone could write that and go on living." I think it was the first time I met Sam, and I felt that someone absolutely extraordinary had come amongst us. I don't think *Endgame* was well received, no Beckett was well received for years and years and years. It was quite different from any kind of theatre that had been done before.

The set for the 1958 production of Endgame.
Photo: Sandra Lousada

Jacques Noel's set was very dour, rather like a tower made of stone. When I came to do the play my design was more abstract and, although I obeyed Sam's instructions, I always felt I hadn't gone away and tried to do anything very personal because I was much too overawed. It's very clear from the text that the dustbins need to be on one side and the door on the other, with the windows each side at the back and very high so as to need a ladder. The French set was completely circular, whilst mine was angular, and I had tall walls that just went on going up, and there were some beams as though it were a kind of ruin. The bricks were a bit cubistic rather than naturalistic, although the chair and the dustbins looked real, and I used dun colours and greys whereas the French set was very much dark grey. I don't remember Sam making any comment on it. It's a play that's so intense that I've always felt it needed to be enclosed and claustrophobic. Some people seem to do it with no walls and I just don't feel that works, especially with the question of climbing up and looking out of the window.

The curious thing about *Endgame* is that it can be very funny. When George and Jackie MacGowran were rehearsing I sometimes used to fetch them from the theatre and drive them home. They'd be rehearsing it in the car and, in amongst the horror and the sheer agony of it all, there was a certain amount of humour coming out, although Sam didn't encourage it in the final performance.

Jackie was a marvellous Clov, and George sometimes gave wonderful performances as Hamm. I used to go and settle him in his chair and put the handkerchief over his face, and he was literally shaking with terror because of the piece. It is a frightening part to play because you're blind and have to have your eyes shut, and you're stuck in a chair all evening.

Below left *George Devine (Hamm) and Jack MacGowran (Clov) in* Endgame.
Photo: anon

Below *Costume drawing for Hamm.*

Krapp's Last Tape

Samuel Beckett, *Directors:* Donald McWhinnie & George Devine
28 October 1958, The Royal Court Theatre (world première).

Beckett asks for Krapp's den, a room with a small two-drawered table, a tape recorder and a microphone, cardboard boxes, a door and darkness.

JH: Our *Krapp* was the first performance ever. When Sam Beckett first wrote it he described Krapp as looking more like a clown and I remember doing a clown-like drawing, but when he saw it he didn't really like it so we just made Krapp an old man in raggedy clothes; he wasn't exactly a tramp, he had fairly formal clothes that had gone to seed, very shiny black trousers that didn't fit well, an old shirt and an old waistcoat.

The set has to be in blacks[1] with a small door at the back, stage right, where he goes to fetch the tapes and have his drink. He has a table with drawers in it, a chair, and a lamp over the table. It's really a question of making sure all the elements are right and not mucking about with it. It should be in darkness except for the light over the table and coming in through the door.

The physical actions are important in all Beckett's plays. In the original script we were working from, Krapp made several journeys off through the curtain at the back to have a drink and to fetch first the ledger, then the tins containing the spools and then the tape recorder which he plugged in. When he found the right tape he swept the rest off the table. All these physical things should be done in silence, perhaps with a few grunts. It's all part of getting ready for the actual play, which is in fact the tape that has already been rehearsed – the tape is all Krapp's voice, and the rest of the play is him listening to himself. If these actions are not done completely truthfully and are overacted or clowned up the play just doesn't work.

In 1973 Anthony Page directed Albert Finney in *Krapp* at The Royal Court. Sam came to a run-through and after the performance he said it wasn't quite what he had in mind and could he show them? He got up and did the whole play on stage. I couldn't move, it was an amazing thing to witness. His timing, the poetry of it, the way he walked, the way he listened, the way he moved was beautiful. I've never seen anybody play it like that again.

1 *Soft or framed black serge or velour which masks the acting area of the stage.*

Costume drawings showing Krapp's progress from clown to the character Beckett preferred.

Krapp's Last Tape.

Roots

Arnold Wesker, *Director:* John Dexter

25 May 1959, Belgrade Theatre, Coventry. The production transferred to The Royal Court Theatre on 30 June and to The Duke of York's Theatre on 30 July 1959 (world première).

The play is set in Norfolk. Act 1 asks for the interior of a ramshackle house. Act 2 moves to the 'neat and ordinary' kitchen of a tied cottage on a main road where part of the garden is visible. Act 3 takes place in the front room of the same cottage. Jocelyn later designed Chicken Soup With Barley *and* I'm Talking About Jerusalem, *the remaining plays in Wesker's* Trilogy.

JH: When we did *Roots* we didn't know it would be part of a trilogy. It is written about the family of Arnold Wesker's wife, Dusty, so I went up to Norfolk with Dusty and Arnold to meet them and see where and how they lived. What was so extraordinary was that the place, the people and their conversation were identical to the text. We went to her sister's cottage, and it was literally down a path and in the middle of a wood. There was a large stove and that's what gave me the idea of basing the whole set round a big chimney stack; all those cottages tend to be built round fireplaces or stoves and chimneys.

It was the first naturalistic play I'd done and the problem was to do it in a non-heavy way, especially since it had three sets. I only had eighty pounds to spend and we kept within the budget, but I remember we weren't able to afford an outside lavatory and a clothes line that we wanted and which would have cost an extra five pounds. The design was a breakthrough in a way, my first attempt at poetic realism for a naturalistic play. I hit on the idea of setting it in the middle of an empty stage and using projections of the countryside. In those days I painted all the projections myself on glass, one for each projector. I was trying to create the *feeling* of those isolated cottages without *actually* re-creating them on stage.

I took the model down to the paint-shop. I thought I had explained it properly, but when I went to see what they'd made I found it was disastrous. The set had been painted like a pantomime and all the wallpapers were double-sized and the wooden doors had been painted to look like wood instead of being made of real wood. I was in utter panic. I'd just seen a rehearsal where the actors were actually frying food in the first act and you could smell it cooking, everything was real. I couldn't imagine the pantomime set working with the kind of acting style John Dexter had achieved, so I had to stay up for two nights washing all the paint off the doors and whiting out the walls and re-doing the whole thing.

John Dexter and I felt very much out on a limb and were worried about letting The Royal Court down. People came from Stratford and London for the first night but by that time I was absolutely exhausted and sat through it feeling rather numb. When it was obviously a success the relief was enormous, and the production was to be the beginning of my long working relationship with John.

Later, we worked together on *Chicken Soup With Barley* and *I'm Talking About Jerusalem*. What was rare about *Chicken Soup* was the fragmentation of the set. It had a window and then half a window, whereas, traditionally, there would have been a whole wall. I used projections again for *Chicken Soup* and this time did large drawings that were photographed and made into slides. Subtle drawings with gentle tones often aren't bold enough for a projection after the lights are on it, so I had to do rather vulgar drawings with strong contrasts. These were done to the scale of the backcloth and then photographed from the angle at which the projectors would be set. We used two projectors up on the proscenium, each throwing half of the image diagonally onto the backcloth. They would be adjusted so that the brightest point of each met in the middle to achieve a sharp image and correct any distortion.

I'm Talking About Jerusalem was just one standing set. The problem was to have enough space inside The Court sightlines to play the sections in the barn as well as in the house. With the final model you could legitimately play outside the house and just bring a chair to sit on. Because the set was open it was evocative and made the human beings more vulnerable. Again, there were projections to show the landscape altering as the seasons changed.

Drawings for Acts 1 & 2 of Roots.

Facing page *Drawing for Act 3 of* Roots.

Above *Act 2* Roots. *For Act 2 the window from the previous act was moved and set at an angle and a different door was moved into the frame. The chimney (stage left Act 1) swung round to a more dominant position.*

Right *Act 1* Roots.

Far right *Act 3* Roots. *The chimney was centred and a door flat and window flat were set in front. A stormy sky was projected onto the cyc.*
Photos: Sandra Lousada

Above *Set photograph for* Chicken Soup With Barley, *Act 1, showing projection upstage.*

Left *Photo of the model for* I'm Talking About Jerusalem.
Photos: Sandra Lousada

ROOTS

The Kitchen

Arnold Wesker, *Director:* John Dexter

6 September 1959, The Royal Court Theatre (world première). First full production 27 June 1961, The Royal Court Theatre.

The play takes place in the kitchen of the Tivoli Restaurant, and the set must provide ovens, tables and serving points whilst creating space for a cast of thirty two to move at speed. The Kitchen *was first seen as one of The Court's 'Sunday night without decor' performances and later given a full production.*

JH: *The Kitchen* had a big impact. Movement is very important in nearly all Arnold Wesker's best plays (in *Roots* it is Beatie's dance) and in this the speed and rhythm of the meal being served were tremendously exciting after all the personal problems earlier in the play. Arnold had written *The Kitchen* before the *Trilogy*, only it was such a big cast nobody could do it. This was John Dexter's first real staging, when you saw what he could do. He could pick up ideas very quickly; staging very much interests him and he has got better and better at it.

I didn't do a model for this. The great thing was that we used the bare stage for the first time with the back wall and all the pipes showing. It was a real breakthrough and I think it was also the first

Set for The Kitchen, *showing back wall and lighting-grid.*
Photo: Peter Smith

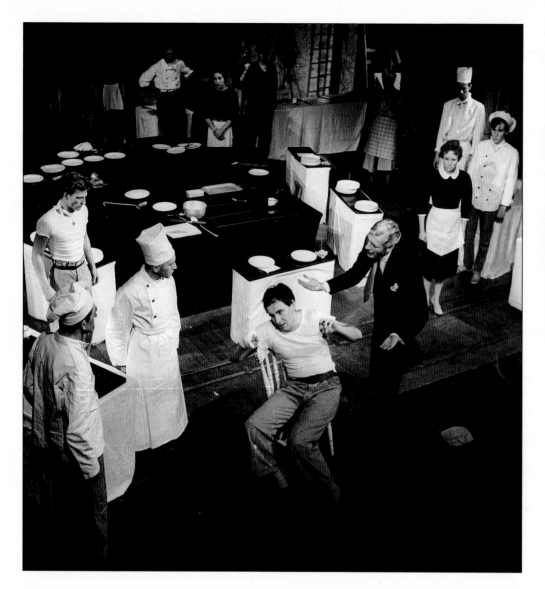

time we put the lighting-rig above the set and allowed everything to be seen. John had the idea of using the lights for the gas; the old man came in and turned on the gas and one by one the lights came on very low and you heard the noise of the gas getting louder and louder as the lights went up.

The central placing of the stoves was obviously essential and the other elements just had to take their positions around it. For the first Sunday performance we used trestle-tables for the stoves and put black-out material over them. The serving points were made of orange-boxes and we put tin on top of them so they made the right noise. The boxes set round the stoves created a passage way; the cook stood in between the boxes and the stoves, and the waitresses came round outside the boxes with their orders. I remember arriving that Sunday and thinking that the tables for the salads and the sweets should be white, so I went home and got my sheets and pinned them round. We never changed the main idea after that, we just made it better.

John Dexter: For Sunday night productions at The Court some of the responsibility and weight was taken off you. Everyone knew there wasn't going to be scenery so you could chance something like *The Kitchen*. You could risk doing with nothing. *The Kitchen* pointed me in the direction – not of minimalism, that's the wrong word – but of provoking the audience to think for themselves and use their imagination.

Above *The George Devine Award benefit performance at The Old Vic. The cast included Sybil Thorndike, Joan Greenwood, Barbara Hicks and Robert Stephens.*
Photos: anon

Above left *The set in action.*
Photo: Sandra Lousada

Serjeant Musgrave's Dance

John Arden, *Director*: Lindsay Anderson
22 October 1959, The Royal Court Theatre (world première).

The eight scenes demand a canal wharf; the bar of a public house; a churchyard; a street; a pub stable and bedroom; a market-place and a prison cell. Arden deliberately does not give a date for the play's setting, but the costumes in this production were typical of the years 1860-80. This was the first time that Jocelyn collaborated with Lindsay Anderson.

Costume drawing for Serjeant Musgrave (Ian Bannen).

JH: *Musgrave* is a wide-reaching play and raised large issues. It has to be played by an absolutely impassioned man and if you don't feel the madness and passion it doesn't work. It was Lindsay Anderson's first big production and I didn't know anything much about him then. We met and he said, "I can't make head or tail of this, how on earth are we going to do it?" – he always said that in those days. We talked to John Arden and I did some drawings.

There are so many scenes in *Musgrave* that it seemed to me you had to do it with very little so as not to have over-long scene changes and lose the urgency of the text. When I work with very little, it's not just an obsession, it's usually a way of coping with the technical problems involved. The first drawings were more elaborate than the last solution and at the model stage we started with a crane and a barge for the first scene on the canal wharf and gradually got down to nothing but a ground row of weeds and grass.

For the pub scene I finally had just one flat and I arranged the tables and chairs so that they created a room. I think Lindsay found it quite difficult working within those confines. He wasn't experienced enough in the theatre and he needed the security of more scenery to help him. I kept

Above *The canal wharf.*
Above right *The prison bars and projection.*

finding that he had moved the actors outside the imaginary walls of the pub which would have meant we had to light the whole stage and, therefore, destroy the illusion of the room. Lindsay's forte is working with actors rather than staging and, naturally, they took priority over the design. He fights the restrictions of a set that demands a certain usage but, although we had the absolute minimum for each scene in *Musgrave*, once he got the hang of it he used the set very well.

Musgrave was the first time I used polystyrene. When I introduced the idea to the workshops at The Court they were very upset and wanted to use wood. In 1960 when I used metal for *Antigone* the carpenters and painters wouldn't touch it and I had to do the whole thing myself. Workshops are often wary of new materials and feel threatened; it's their whole way of life and you can't blame them. It was quick and easy to make the gravestone for *Musgrave* out of polystyrene. I did rubbings in an old graveyard and just drew them on the polystyrene with a soldering iron and painted it to give it the right texture. For the model I made the big cross out of a mantle from a gas fire which I cut up and we later reproduced it life-size; it conveyed the right feeling but was not naturalistic.

Lindsay Anderson: Being inexperienced in the theatre myself and not particularly avant-garde, Jocelyn frightened me on *Musgrave* by continually removing bits of the set and I got very scared. For instance, in the pub scene first one wall would go and then another wall would go and I remember saying, "There won't be anything left!" That was my timidity and, of course, she was absolutely right. She worked towards a very simplified and austere but strong design.

41

Facing page *Costume drawing for Hurst (Alan Dobie).*

Above and above right *Early drawing for the pub scene and photograph showing the pared-down version that was used in the production.*
Photo: Snowdon

Right *The churchyard.*

The Changeling

Thomas Middleton & William Rowley, *Director:* Tony Richardson
21 February 1961, The Royal Court Theatre.

Written circa 1623, The Changeling *is set in 'Alicant', Spain. It is a five act play, set mainly inside the castle of a nobleman, Vermandero, and on the city streets. The sub-plot demands scenes set in a mad-house.*

JH: I used to get more and more infuriated with Tony Richardson because he took no notice of George Devine's and my feelings about the sets not having elaborate designs. In 1957 Tony directed *The Making of Moo* and when I saw the set I refused to paint it. At the dress rehearsal I said to the author, Nigel Dennis, "Did you mean it to look like this?" and, of course, he hadn't even noticed. It very often doesn't occur to writers to imagine what their plays will look like. Tony didn't speak to me for about two years and asking me to do *The Changeling* was a sort of burying the hatchet. I was preparing for *Richard III* at Stratford and he persuaded me to do just the set for him and to let someone else do the costumes, which is something I normally never do.

The set was a very, very simple thing. This was the second time I used just the bare stage and the back wall, and the only thing I added was one textured white flat at the back with a doorway in it. The doors were beautifully carved and could be left either open or closed. For the interior of Vermandero's house we lowered the beams, which were hinged to the front of the flat, and which threw interesting shadows. For the scene in his daughter's bedroom I made a screen by cutting out folded paper in a pattern and attaching it to sticks of bamboo so that it had a strange, Spanish look to it, and we made a beautiful seat which, again, was taken from Spanish paintings. To achieve the mad-house we flew in an awning, like matting, and added a grille to the doorway. Then three traps came up, also with grilles, so that the madmen seemed to be in pens behind them.

Tony Richardson: *The Changeling* was based on Goya. It was an extremely successful piece of design, with a very simple, stark, rough white wall and realistic period costumes. I think I came up with the idea of using Goya and Jocelyn suggested the white wall. That's the kind of collaboration we had, I would come up with a basic style for the play and staging and she would find ways of imaginatively presenting it to an audience.

Left *Interior, central flat with door and beams.*
Middle *Interior, using cut-out screen.*
Below *Mad-house, showing the scrim awning. Bars replaced the door and stood round the trap openings.*
Photos: Sandra Lousada

Luther

John Osborne, *Director:* Tony Richardson

26 June 1961, The production previewed at The Theatre Royal Nottingham before opening at The Royal Court Theatre 27 July 1961 and transferring to The Phoenix Theatre on 5 September 1961 (world première).

The play is set in the sixteenth century and calls for the Convent of the Augustinian Order of Eremites at Erfurt; the market place at Jütebog; the Eremite Cloister at Wittenberg; the steps of the Castle Church, Wittenberg; the Fugger Palace, Augsburg; a hunting lodge in Magliana, Italy; The Elster Gate, Wittenberg; The Diet of Worms.

Drawing for the interior of the monastery.

JH: *Luther* was the first visually big show that I'd designed for The Court. The text had an absolute vibrancy and was a wonderful mixture of Osborne and Luther. Our first nights at The Court were always exciting because we never knew whether the audience would like a play or just walk out, and it was extraordinary to see a work like *Luther* in that theatre. I always felt this was a very good production and I don't remember having any qualms about it.

Tony Richardson was full of ideas and very brilliant and inspiring, and John Osborne produced some sheets of marvellous medieval German woodcuts. I found books about Luther and the Popes – all the details I used of the Papal coat of arms and decorations came from illustrations. I enjoy researching and I like to use what I find in a theatrical rather than a naturalistic way.

I think the influence I had on the production was in creating a space so that we could have room both for the monastery and the exteriors. I used a series of huge flats across the back wall, looking like a complete cloth, with texture on them. I put plaster on the model and then scored and painted it. It appeared to be abstract Gothic arches going into the distance with a floor of receding stone slabs. This provided a medieval background to the whole production and the arches gave the feeling of being connected to the church. The back wall and the floor were stone coloured and the colours for *Luther* were mainly dark greens, blacks and gold. For the richer scenes I used gauzes, based on pictures from books, in bright oranges, reds and golds, which, as well as being transparent, could be lit as if they were solid.

Above *Sketches for the noviciate ceremony.*

46

Photograph showing the permanent back wall of textured arches and the paved wall. Here seen with the branch used to create the monastery garden. Photo: *Sandra Lousada*

One of the most exciting moments is seeing your set going up on stage looking exactly like the model. I made a very complex *Luther* model which the workshop built and painted. If you make a model that really works and is carefully painted and made to scale then, unless you get hopeless construction people and painters, it actually does look the same on stage. A good scene painter is able to interpret what a designer wants on a much larger scale – occasionally it's disappointing but very often they improve it.

Sets are meant to be peopled, and lighting is terribly important, but with the model you can only imagine how the lighting might be – you may have an idea without knowing exactly how it can be achieved. In the old days at The Court we didn't have any lighting designers and George Devine always lit the plays he directed with the lighting engineers. Lighting designers are best when they start as lighting engineers and it's only in America that they're allowed a free hand to light as they like with no collaboration with the designer and, often, the director. I've never worked like that, and I wouldn't, because a lighting designer needs to be able to collaborate with the director and designer as much as anyone else involved in the production. Theatre is the collaboration of many different talents to serve the play and the actors.

It was possible to contain the acting area in *Luther* by putting in a small element and lighting only

that part of the stage. To change the atmosphere we just added a table and chairs or flew in a tree when we needed a garden. The tree was an indication of a tree, a rather old, dead one, and it was made of wire and covered in canvas. When Luther made his speech to the Diet of Worms we simply brought in a pulpit and flew in the symbol of the Pope and the Medicis. The burning of books was done using lights to throw flames against the back wall. I based the Christ figure on the Grünewald Christ in the monastery at Isenheim and carved it out of polystyrene. It was massive, about three times the size of a human being, and very exaggerated and tortured; at some points in the play it was high in the air and at others it was lowered.

The austerity of the monastery was actually very beautiful, the monotonous background gave a framework where anything could happen. The mixture of austerity and richness was dictated by the text; the citizens and peasants were very plain, dark and sombre whereas the Papal scenes and those with the cardinals were rich and opulent and their clothes were made of velvet and silk. I used simplified costumes of the period and was able to get a lot of the quality of them by buying patterned material, bleaching and dyeing it and then painting it before it was cut – it's the kind of experimenting I enjoy. The point of dyeing fabric is to get a not too perfect dye which gives dark and light variations to the material.

Facing page *The Christ figure.*
This page above *The Diet of Worms.*
Above right *The noviciate ceremony.*
Photos: Sandra Lousada

Chips With Everything

Arnold Wesker, *Director:* John Dexter
27 April 1962, The Royal Court Theatre (world première).

Chips With Everything *is set at an R.A.F. station in England and requires both the exterior and interior of an R.A.F. hut, with several full-length beds visible in the interior. Other scenes take place on the parade ground, on a roadway, inside a lecture hall and in the NAAFI.*

JH: Some plays are more visually exciting to do and others are more technically challenging; the interesting thing about sets is solving the problems. This was more of a technical problem, but it was also a visual problem to create the feeling of a group of people in the space of an airfield on The Court stage – The Court always dictated the proportions of every set.

   Chips is very much an inside/outside play. I immediately visualised a huge cyc and a tall red and white striped pole, and I went to visit an airfield to see the sort of huts they had and the guardroom with the fire buckets and other details. The main problem was the hut and the difficulty of the beds. The exterior of the hut had to be seen in the parade ground, and it also had to open up and to have beds inside which would be long enough for the actors to lie down on. I thought of making extendable beds and had to find out if that was technically possible. Then John Dexter got the idea of the soldiers drilling to overcome the problem of opening the hut, and in the end the drilling went right the way through the play and he got someone from the army to come and instruct the actors. The designer always has to solve the problems somehow, although you may not solve them to your satisfaction. I think this was one of the better ones.

John Dexter: I knew the drilling would be paramount, it was at the heart of the play. I remembered National Service and that drilling was miserable.

Arnold Wesker: I can't see the play being designed in any other way. I've seen a number of productions of it now. One at the Paris TNP was a dreadfully abstract production where the designer played around with shapes that looked like the interior of a modern furniture boutique so that you had 'L' shapes that were couches and beds at one moment and if you propped them up they became arches. It was awful. The other productions have been variations on Jocelyn's design. Her sets were aesthetically satisfying and absolutely in keeping with the spirit of the play and with reality. When people say 'theatre design' to me, *Chips with Everything* and *Serjeant Musgrave* are the sets which loom.

Photographs of scenes from Chips with Everything, *showing the workings of the hut and the beds.*
Photos: Sandra Lousada

Happy Days

Samuel Beckett, *Director: George Devine*
1 November 1962, The Royal Court Theatre (first production in English).

Beckett's stage directions ask for an "expanse of scorched grass rising centre to low mound. Gentle slopes down to front and either side of stage. Back an abrupter fall to stage level. Maximum of simplicity and symmetry. Blazing light. Very pompier trompe-l'oeil backcloth to represent unbroken plain and sky receding to meet in far distance." The two acts are virtually a monologue spoken by Winnie, who is embedded up to her waist in the mound during Act 1 and up to her neck in Act 2. Act 1 requires Winnie's parasol to ignite.

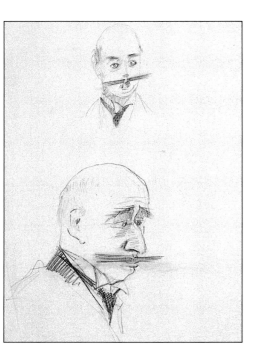

Facing page *Drawing for Act 1 of* Happy Days.
This page *Sketches of Willie.*

JH: I had a terrible problem with the blue sky which Sam Beckett referred to in the text as being azure. I just couldn't make it work with the yellow sand although I tried three or four different drawings and, eventually, I did one with an orange sky. I sent them all to Sam and said did he think orange was better because it gave the idea of more concentrated heat? He wrote back and agreed, and from then on *Happy Days* was done with an orange sky.

The mound I did for this was a failure as far as I was concerned. In the drawings I had a perspective of sand dunes going away, but in the theatre you could really only see it properly from the Circle because the mound got in the way. Unfortunately it was too egg-shaped, and it should have been covered so that it wasn't so smooth but somehow that never got done. Winnie's chair was on a trap so that it could be lowered for the second half. I don't think it's uncomfortable for whoever plays Winnie, she can move her arms around underneath in the second half and there's usually a bar to hold on to.

The parasol was murder, but we got it working beautifully in the end, using litmus paper. It had to burst into flames and when Winnie threw it over her shoulders it had to go out as she said, "Ah earth you old extinguisher." There were two parasols: Winnie dropped the first parasol and Willie appeared to hand it back but he actually handed back one with a battery and switch on it.

This page *Brenda Bruce as Winnie. Act 1 (above) Act 2 (left).*
Photos: Zoë Dominic

Facing page *Billie Whitelaw as Winnie in the 1979 production (Act 2).*
Photo: John Haynes

Happy Days

Samuel Beckett, *Director:* Samuel Beckett
7 June 1979, The Royal Court Theatre.

For set details see 1962 production.

JH: The second time I did *Happy Days* the mound was more elaborate and layered. I think Sam Beckett had changed his attitude to the mound too and thought we should have it more broken up with bits coming off it. It's important that the set provides a complete void and gives the impression of unremitting heat. If the mound for the first production was too simple, this one was too elaborate. Sam decided that the parasol should only smoulder and go black rather than go up in flames as it did before, and that was rather more difficult to organise. It was always a terror to know whether it was going to work or not.

Samuel Beckett: I remember shocking Jocelyn when we did *Happy Days* with Billie Whitelaw. Billie was wonderful as usual, but it is a terribly difficult play and in one rehearsal I said, "I'm beginning to hate this play." I felt I couldn't bear the text anymore. Jocelyn reproached me for saying that in front of Billie.

Billie Whitelaw as Winnie. Act 2.
Photo: John Haynes

Exit The King

Eugene Ionesco (translated by Donald Watson), *Director:* George Devine
12 September 1963, The Royal Court Theatre.

The action takes place in the dilapidated throne-room of a crumbling palace which gradually becomes more derelict as the play progresses. At the end the doors, windows and walls of the room are seen to disappear or collapse. Two of the thrones have to disappear during the performance and the third needs to be set on a revolving rostrum so that the King can vanish at the end.

Costume drawing for Berenger (Alec Guinness).

JH: *Various characters have to disappear very suddenly during the action and we made use of The Court's star traps (a trap in the stage floor on which an actor or a prop can appear or disappear very quickly) to achieve this. The play is about different aspects of death and decay and was called surreal and absurd. Most of Ionesco's plays work best within a framework of realism which allows the astonishment of what happens to achieve its full impact.*

Above *Sketch for* Exit the King.

Far left *Photograph of the model.*
Photo: anon

Left *Production photograph of Alec Guinness as Berenger.*
Photo: Sandra Lousada

The Seagull

Anton Chekhov (translated by Ann Jellicoe), *Director: Tony Richardson*
12 March 1964, The ESC at The Queen's Theatre.

Chekhov's four act play demands: the park of an estate where a rough stage has been erected in front of a lake; the croquet lawn and flowerbeds of the estate with the house and terrace; the dining room of the house; the drawing room of the house which has been converted into a study.

Costume drawings for The Seagull.

Dr Dorn in "The Seagull" - 1964.

Jocelyn Herbert.

Costume drawings for The Seagull.

Production photograph of George Devine (Dorn) and Peggy Ashcroft (Arkadina).
Photo: Sandra Lousada

JH: Michel Saint-Denis talked a lot about Chekhov at the London Theatre Studio, about the importance of the company feeling, how every part, however small, should be played by a great actor and how important the details of the props were. I think the first Chekhov I saw was the *Three Sisters* which Michel directed in 1938 with John Gielgud, Alec Guinness and Peggy Ashcroft. George Devine played Andrey and also did the lighting, and it was designed by the Motleys. When the Stanislavski Theatre came from Russia [the Moscow Arts Theatre brought *The Cherry Orchard* and *Three Sisters* to Sadler's Wells in 1958] we all went to see the great masters. The performances were good, but I had a sense of disappointment having seen Michel's *Three Sisters*. Michel had tried poetic realism rather than naturalism and, after that, the Russian sets seemed very old fashioned to us, very much tatty painted scenery.

For *The Seagull* I tried to find a design that fitted my ideas of not having it too naturalistic; there's a difference between reproducing the real thing and giving a poetic indication of it. I had been to Russia in 1937, and I'd read a lot about Stanislavski's theatre. Russian country houses were wooden with balconies and terraces, and I did a lot of research into their interiors, which tended to have Victorian furniture. The inside/outside is very important in *The Seagull*. I used the feeling of slatted houses like the dachas in the countryside. The garden was just a tree and a painted backcloth of birch trees and the lake – birch trees are somehow the symbol of Russia. When I was working on the tree I first made it by cutting folded paper and making holes, then I found some material and experimented with it and it really looked quite like a silver birch. There was an awful problem about fire-proofing the leaves – there always was in those days with trees – now it's easy because you just dunk the material in fire-proofing liquid. The backcloth was filled gauze so that as the moon came up you saw it rising above the lake until it reached an unpainted space in the gauze where it shone through.

Above *The garden.*

Facing page above *The Dining Room.* Below *The Study.* *The backcloth and tree remained on stage throughout* The Seagull. *For the interior scenes the tree was moved upstage and the slatted wall with French doors and windows showing the terrace outside was flown in. A slatted false pros was flown downstage which, with furniture, created the sense of a room. For the last act the blinds were replaced by heavy curtains.*
Photos: John Cook

For the dining room we flew in a flat which had pale curtains and blinds on golden-silvery slatted wood and you could see the tree outside through gaps in the slats. The next act is in the drawing room so I just put different furniture in it and put in heavy velvet curtains with flowers on them instead of the blinds. The furniture was solid, heavy Russian furniture but the walls were pale like bleached wood.

The play takes place during the summer and most of the costumes were pale colours. There are always one or two which take a while and in this production Masha took a bit of getting right because one tended to make her too nun-like but in the end I made her – not seductive – but less severe.

Design of the painting for the backwall of the ESC's production of Saint Joan of the Stockyards *at The Queen's Theatre.*

Saint Joan of the Stockyards

Bertolt Brecht (translated by Charlotte & A.L. Lloyd), *Director:* Tony Richardson
11 June 1964, ESC at The Queen's Theatre.

Scenes take place in the Chicago Stockyards; in front of the Lennox plant; in a street; in front of the Black Straw Hats' Mission; in front of the Livestock Market; in the Stockyards District; inside Sullivan Slift's house in the City; in Mauler's office; in a little tavern in the Stockyards District; in front of the Graham Company Storehouse; in the environs of Graham's Warehouse.

JH: *Joan of the Stockyards* is a difficult play and very elaborate – there are so many scenes and so many different elements. I read some extraordinary books about the Chicago meat market – Kipling went to Chicago and wrote devastatingly about it – and I was sent horrifying pictures from America.

At first I thought the design would be more like a stockyard so I did masses of drawings for that, but I was still left with the problem of all the scenes needing to change quickly.

In those days I was keen on using the back wall and setting things in the middle of the stage, and I made an enormous collage of the stockyards that went from wall to wall at the back so the audience was aware of it all the time. In the end I solved the problem of the scene changes by using triangular periaktois[1] which turned both up and downstage. There was someone inside each one with a scene change light and they could just swivel round, so each periaktoi had three different surfaces that could be used in different combinations and they were very flexible and quick. It took a while to get them right, but they worked very well. I built the stage out and we lit only the centre area. Two downstage ramps led up to the set so we could use them to move props on and off, and we just flew in whatever extra elements were needed. It was an unusual design for that time and it really did solve a problem.

Tony Richardson needed singers in the production and they were also supposed to double as meat-packers. Very early on I suggested putting them in masks, but he said, "I don't want anything like that, nothing arty. No masks". The singers just couldn't act, and about a week before we were due to

Across two pages, top row from left to right
Street, Slift's House, Outside the factory, Meat market.

Bottom row
Outside the Black Straw Hats' Mission, Office, Canteen, Inside the Black Straw Hats' Mission.

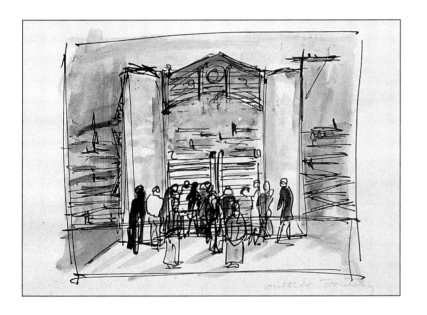

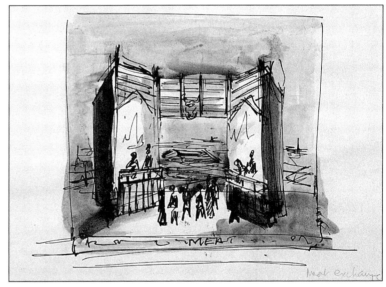

Facing page and this page *Production photographs showing the periaktois in different positions.* Photos: anon

open Tony was in despair so I suggested masks again and he agreed. I rushed home and got Jenny, my daughter, and an assistant and we made all the masks – well over fifty – in my kitchen at Rossetti Studios. I'd only ever made one leather mask before, but I had an idea that it might work if I made a mould and put the leather on and baked it and then painted and varnished it. The masks were very simple, just jowls a bit like a pig, and the make-up was the same colour as they were. They were like putting on a glove so they didn't get in the singers' way and they worked like a charm. Mostly, the moment people put on masks they think they're not seen, so their bodies are liberated; it's a completely unconscious response.

Tony Richardson: *Joan* was a disaster for several reasons, partly because we had to make major cast changes but also because it was ahead of its time and people weren't prepared to see that kind of anti-capitalist work done in a capitalist theatre – it was a kind of dichotomy they couldn't deal with. Visually it was stunning, and it's a great pity that more people didn't see Jocelyn's design.

I've always hated masks and my eyes glaze over when Jocelyn or Peter Brook start talking about how much more expressive they are. If you have stupid faces and the figures are meant to be abstract then I can see the point of a mask, but I don't buy the idea that someone acts better in a mask – but that can be my prejudice. With *Joan* I had about sixty singers on stage who were also supposed to play stockbrokers and different groups of people, and I realised they were hopeless beyond belief so at the last minute I saw that the only thing to do was to put them in half-masks.

Facing page *Costume drawings.*

Above *Half-mask drawing for* Saint Joan of the Stockyards.

1 *Periaktoi: a three (or more) sided structure on a pivot which turns to reveal a different side to the audience, thus creating a new scene.*

Julius Caesar

William Shakespeare, *Director:* Lindsay Anderson
26 November 1964, The Royal Court Theatre.

The play requires: a street in Rome; Brutus' orchard; Caesar's house; the Capitol; the Forum; a room in Anthony's house; Brutus' tent at a camp near Sardis; the Plains of Philippi.

Facing page, left column from top
Rome exterior, showing permanent textured back flat and steps and the metal statue, the symbol of Caesar.

The Storm.

Tent scene.

Right column
The Capitol, Caesar's seat with pillars flown in.

The fire.

Detail of the wall in Brutus' garden.

This page below *The battle symbol.*
Photos: Zoë Dominic

JH: From the design point of view this was an attempt at what Lindsay Anderson calls poetic realism and the scenic elements were sculptural and indicative of mood more than place. We attempted a basic costume, but we didn't get it right. *Caesar* was beautifully directed and there were some very good performances but, alas, it was not a success.

A Patriot for Me

John Osborne, *Director:* Anthony Page
30 June 1965, The Royal Court Theatre (world première).

The text asks for: a gymnasium of the 7th Galician Infantry Regiment at Lemburg, Galicia in 1890; the office of the Commandant; a private cubicle at a club, Anna's; an upstairs bedroom at Anna's; a darkened office in Warsaw; a terrace in the Hofburg, the Emperor's residence in Vienna; the drawing room at the home of Countess Delyanoff; Oblensky's office; a café; a bare darkened room with a bed; a ballroom in Vienna in 1902; a lecture room; a hill clearing outside Dresden, surrounded by fir trees; Redl's baroque and luxurious apartment in Vienna; the Red Lounge at the Sacher Hotel, Vienna; a hospital ward; a hotel room near the Polish border in Galicia; Redl's apartment in Prague; Redl's bedroom at the Hotel Klomser; the street outside the Hotel Klomser; a Chamber of Deputies, Vienna.

At the time of this production homosexual acts between consenting male adults were still illegal in Britain (the Sexual Offences Act became law in 1967). The Lord Chamberlain asked for three scenes to be deleted and The Royal Court was turned into a club theatre to avoid having to make these cuts. Members of the ESC were active in campaigning for an end to censorship.

JH: *Patriot* had twenty scenes so had to be done with the minimum amount of props and scenery. I used side flats which swung on and off and each had three revolving panels that could be changed for the different scenes and which could be set at different angles and didn't need to be always symmetrical. I solved the other problems using projections.

I did a lot of research on the play and Tony Page and I went over to Vienna with the actor playing Redl, Maximilian Schell. We used to go to the opera and then to nightclubs and see all the young men with ancient ladies and the old men with beautiful girls all dressed up to the nines. Tony and I used to sit trying to persuade Schell that Redl's homosexuality was really important because he didn't think that it was and was afraid of it. Until George Devine agreed to play the part of the Drag Queen (which John Osborne had written for him) no-one would do the play because of its homosexuality. Once George said he'd do it, casting was plain sailing. It was wonderful listening to Ferdie singing Figaro at the beginning of the second act and then George would turn round dressed as Queen Alexandra and say, "Well done, Ferdie," and the audience would realise who it was and fall about because it was so unexpected.

The whole theatre was turned upside down because it was such a large cast and we had to make dressing rooms under the stage and anywhere we could. George dressed in his office at the top of the building and used to sail through the secretary's room in his high heels and corsets smoking a cigar saying, "Excuse me, I'm just going to the Ladies."

Facing page Sets showing the projections in use.
This page top Projection drawing.
Left Set showing use of the side flats.
Photos: Zoë Dominic

BARON

This page *Costume drawing and production photograph of The Baron (George Devine).*
Photo Zoë Dominic

Facing page above left *Costume drawing for General Conrad von Hotzendorf (Sebastian Shaw).*

Above right *Costume drawing for Redl (Maximilian Schell).*

Right *Costume drawing for a guest at the Baron's ball.*

Right middle *Costume drawing for Godiva.*

Far right *Suzanna.*

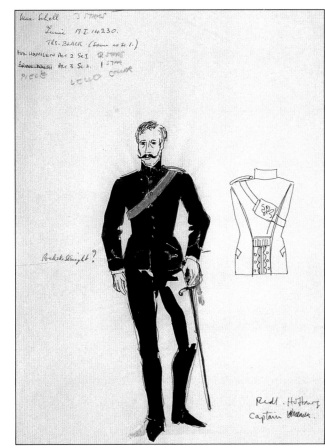

Three Months Gone

Donald Howarth, *Director:* Ronald Eyre
28 January 1970, The Royal Court Theatre, transferred to The Duchess Theatre 4 March 1970 (world première).

The action takes place in the main room of a bungalow. Doors to the bathroom, the front door and the bedrooms open off from the hall which is visible during the performance and which leads into the main room. A glazed door leads into the garden lean-to which also serves as an entrance to the kitchen which can be seen through a hatch.

JH: *Three Months Gone* was a strange play, naturalistic and a bit surreal, so it had to have a heightened style. The problem was to provide a suburban bungalow where the action demanded that you could see people in the kitchen, in the sitting room, coming from the front door and in the corridor to all the bedrooms. It needed a lot of doors and space for people to keep coming in and out with different things happening. It was a technical problem, and the question was to find a way to do it which wasn't boring.

The solution we found was to create the structure of the house with a series of cut-cloths, and to build the interior angles. The fact that it was real and not real worked in a funny way; the wallpaper was blown up to double size but the furniture was real. I felt the play needed this kind of treatment and I wanted it to have a certain amount of claustrophobia.

Production photograph showing the interior of the bungalow. Photo: anon

Come and Go

Samuel Beckett, *Director: Bill Gaskill*

31 March 1970, Theatre Upstairs at The Royal Court Theatre. (The play was presented in a programme entitled Beckett/3 which also included Cascando *and* Play.*)*

The play requires a bench and two black screens.

JH: *Come and Go* is a lovely piece. The three women sit on the bench like butterflies. They have a light over their heads and they wear white gloves and hats with large brims and veils that cast big shadows over their faces. The play needs a black screen on each side of the bench behind which they disappear when they go off from the stage and from which they emerge when they come back. Each goes out in turn. At the end they're all on the bench holding hands as the light fades. We had a wind machine to blow the veils.

The things Sam Beckett has written are amazingly varied. He has such a specific feeling about the rhythm of his words and the pauses, it's all so musically orientated. Fewer and fewer people have seen the old productions and they don't know how to do them as he intended – or worse still, they don't want to do them as he intended.

Home

David Storey, *Director:* Lindsay Anderson
17 June 1970, The Royal Court Theatre, transferred to The Apollo Theatre 29 July 1970 (world première).

The stage directions of Home *ask for a bare stage on which are placed a round metalwork table and two metalwork chairs.*

JH: David Storey's plays reveal the utter frailty of people and how caught they are in their own particular little worlds or nets, like a kaleidoscope. He can make a poem out of the trivia of human life and has a quality of putting people on stage and letting them reveal themselves sometimes with just a few lines. I'm sure David is a completely isolated person, and in a strange way he's near to Beckett. I suppose I find these people the ones I respond to most, the ones who are isolated and alone and with whom you have rare moments of communication.

For *Home* there was a stage direction saying that there shouldn't be any set, but actually there did have to be something. At one point I was going to make it more institutionalised, with very rigid paths, but gradually we realised we needed less and less. I made a model and we put the white table and chairs on it and Lindsay Anderson said, "We must have a flagstaff," and became absolutely obsessive about it – and he was right. Then he felt it would be good to have someone raised up a bit, so we put in the walkway at the back with its two steps down. We decided it was an old place and that's why we added the broken balustrade. Lindsay doesn't like working in the abstract, but he can make do with very little once he feels happy with it.

It was quite an achievement to get John Gielgud and Ralph Richardson to play *Home* and they were a bit nervous. I persuaded them both to be their own age and not wear toupees, and I got John out of his smart suits and Ralph into a jacket that didn't quite fit; it took a lot of doing. They both became more and more enamoured of the play and they and Dandy Nichols and Mona Washbourne were wonderful in it. I loved that production, it was sheer joy.

Facing page *Early sketches for* Home.

Photo right: John Haynes

HARRY

"Home" John Gielgud.

KATHLEEN

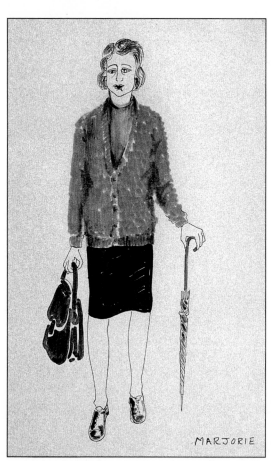

MARJORIE

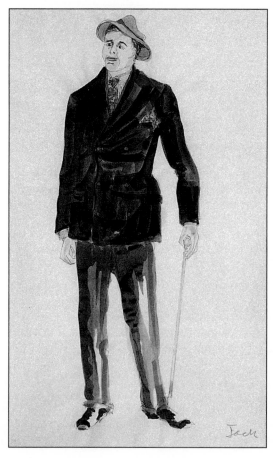

Jack

Facing page top *Production photograph of Mona Washbourne (Kathleen) and Dandy Nichols (Marjorie).*

Above *The fit-up for* Home. *Jocelyn Herbert can be seen inspecting the balustrade.*

Far right *Production photograph of Ralph Richardson (Jack) and John Gielgud (Harry).*

The empty set at The Royal Court.
Photos: John Haynes

This page top far left *Costume drawing for Harry (John Gielgud);* top left *Costume drawing for Kathleen (Mona Washbourne);* bottom far left *Costume drawing for Marjorie (Dandy Nichols);* bottom left *Costume drawing for Jack (Ralph Richardson).*

Lindsay Anderson: David Storey had asked that there shouldn't be a set, but I didn't think that was adequate. The moment you ask for chairs someone has to decide *which* chairs. It's very difficult, as Jocelyn would be the first to admit, to do a play without a set, and the fewer things on stage the more difficult it is. To ask for an empty stage is dangerous, after all which theatre will the play be done in? An empty stage can sometimes look a bit arty and I didn't want that.

I'm proud of the flagstaff we had in *Home*. Both Jocelyn and David fought it strongly but I just felt it had to be there. Often the reasons you're given against any particular idea may be totally irrational. The flagstaff was a good idea because it was plastically correct, a good vertical line, which was important, and because it was symbolically correct and worked at the end of the play: if you have a flagstaff it implies a flag.

David Storey: I'd asked for no set except the table and the chairs. Jocelyn had, I was told, a sentimental addiction to a bare stage and so there was an immediate rapport. Lindsay, however, is a very concrete director to whom abstraction is anathema. Our discussions round Jocelyn's model of the empty box with the little table and chairs were very helpful. Jocelyn has enormous artistic generosity; some designers go pale and feel threatened if anyone makes a suggestion but with her suggestions are treated warmly and positively encouraged.

Even with a terrace and two steps behind it the set was still pretty abstract and I probably resisted even those, preferring to focus absolutely on the characters. I had a totally impractical notion of theatre in terms of audiences and had no idea how to get people to sit and watch two chairs and a table for the whole evening. I didn't consider the audience at all, so the set for *Home* really grew out of my naivety, Jocelyn's intuition and Lindsay's desire for the plastic and graphic.

The Changing Room

David Storey, *Director:* Lindsay Anderson
9 November 1971, The Royal Court Theatre (world première).

The set is a changing room used by the players of a Rugby League team.

JH: Lindsay Anderson and I went to Wakefield to watch a football match and prowled round the changing room where I made sketches of the baths and hooks and things. It was very valuable to see the massage table and other equipment and how it was used. Later Lindsay sent the cast to Bev Risman (technical advisor to the Rugby League) to be coached and they actually played a game.

I remember making the model and even including the coats and shirts with red and blue stripes. Lindsay and David Storey used to come round and fight over the model and vie with each other to put different bits in, but it all worked itself out in the end. There were three or four stanchions which looked as if they were holding up the stadium at different heights, and the pipes went across the room. The set had the sort of scruffy look that those places have. I don't know why but I was sure it had to be an awful green.

You could see the loo cisterns behind the changing area and the chains being pulled. We actually had a bath offstage big enough for twelve people, so that when the players came in from the match they went into the bath and came out dripping – they loved it. We had to reinforce the floor and solve a few problems to get the water running in and out.

There was great discussion of the colours for the team. Lindsay was at his most irritating over the costumes they wore off the field. He'd say, "Why do you need these drawings, why do you bother? They can wear their own clothes." The fact is that a drawing gives you something to start with even if it gets knocked down, and the actors like it and are unhappy if there isn't a costume drawing. I said that they could wear their own clothes if they wanted to and some did and others preferred not to; in a way it's better if they can because their own are already broken down and look used.

Left *Drawing for* The Changing Room.
Facing page *Production photograph.*
Photo: John Haynes

I thought Lindsay did *The Changing Room* quite beautifully, it was like a marvellous conductor with a beautiful instrument. He never rushes, but very much lets things grow and allows people to find their own characters.

Lindsay Anderson: *The Changing Room* is not exactly a naturalistic play although it might seem so. For example, the dialogue is not naturalistic. There's no talk of money, the match, no coarse language or sexual jokes. The play is like a ballet in terms of choreography, but with every move justified in realistic terms and never seeming to be a move for the sake of movement. It is realistic and poetic in the sense that it is creating a world which has a significance and reverberation beyond the immediately naturalistic.

Jocelyn and I went to a real changing room and determined what we could from the actual thing and then went to work finding a refined, simplified version which would be true to the essential action of the play but not fussing it up with unnecessary detail. David's intimate knowledge of the material of the play and his understanding of the problems of staging were hugely important. The scene with the bath could not have been as well played if the actors were just sponged down by somebody. The degree of liberation and expansiveness that was in the scene was achieved through giving the actors that experience.

David Storey: *The Changing Room* was triggered by seeing *The Contractor* and was inspired by the visual impact of that production. Watching the actors come in and build the tent and go off again, I suddenly had an image of a changing room where people come into the room, which changes by their being in it, and in turn, changes them. Then they depart and the room goes back to being what it was and they return to what they were. It was a vivid image; it was the actors' changing room but since I knew more about football than acting I transposed it to a football changing room and carried on from there. Jocelyn's set was absolutely in tune with the material, very close to what I'd visualised. It wasn't a room I'd been in, but a combination.

Jocelyn Herbert, Lindsay Anderson and David Storey with the model for The Changing Room. *Photo: John Haynes*

Not I

Samuel Beckett, *Director:* Anthony Page
16 January 1973, The Royal Court Theatre (first performance in Britain).

Not I is a torrent of words lasting approximately sixteen minutes. It requires the stage to be in darkness but for the Mouth upstage audience right, about eight feet above stage level. Downstage audience left is a tall, speechless, standing figure enveloped from head to foot in a loose, black, hooded djellaba, placed on an invisible podium about four feet high. In this production the Mouth was played by Billie Whitelaw.

JH: One Christmas George Devine and I went over to Paris and we saw quite a lot of Sam Beckett. On Boxing Day we all met at the Coupole, and we dragged Sam off to see *Exit the King* with Ionesco and afterwards George, Sam, my daughter Jenny and I went from bar to bar until dawn. Sam and George were debating the extent to which you could remove human beings from the stage and still write a dramatic text: the idea of *Not I* was germinating in Sam's mind.

Not I was really a technical problem to find a way to black Billie Whitelaw's face up and light her mouth since the whole point is to have the rest of the face and body invisible. I had a miniature spotlight at the time and I made a model of the play and managed to spot just the mouth and leave the rest all black. Billie wore a black hood and I made a mask from black gauze which fitted exactly. She reddened her lips and we made up the area around them in white so the effect was of a rather enlarged mouth.

I built a big chair and put it up on a rostrum – it was rather like being in an electric chair – and gave Billie something to hold onto at the front so that she didn't fall out. When the theatre first went into darkness she was panic-stricken. We had a low screen in front of the chair so that the audience couldn't see the light and for each performance the bulb was focused on her mouth again. The mouth needed to be high in order to seem to float and be disembodied, and it also had to be at that height so that everybody in the auditorium could see it. Obviously it wasn't good to have Billie bang in the middle because of her relationship with the other figure. The flapping onlooker was on a sort of diving board that projected out from the pros and had a very faint light on him so that he could really only be seen when he raised his arms.

Samuel Beckett: *Not I* is an outburst. Anthony Page said it was too fast and wanted to make it comprehensible. Billie and I won. There was a lot of trouble with the silent observer in the play who has to raise his arms. It's very difficult to get the timing right.

Billie Whitelaw: *Not I* was a play where I really did need moral support, and Jocelyn and Sam were a tower of strength in the auditorium while I was rehearsing. There's such a warmth in Jocelyn, and her presence was very important. I used to bleat to her, "I'm never going to make it," and she was marvellously supportive – after all, it wasn't her problem whether I made it or not.

At first I didn't take Jocelyn's advice and I said I would like to stand up during the performance so that I could bring more energy to it. When I was rehearsing I would practice staring at one spot, driving my thoughts like a laser beam as if I were making a hole in the wall. Of course, all that was taken from me when the lights went out, and I couldn't see the light shining on my mouth because there wasn't a beam. I was standing on a raised platform and when I tried to speak standing in the pitch dark I got raging vertigo and sensory deprivation and began to hyperventilate. I tried to keep going but suddenly I stepped outside myself and couldn't control what my body was doing any more. I was convinced I was tumbling over and over in space like an astronaut, and then I broke down. I was dizzy and blacked out. I believe it is a means of torture to play white sound and put black bags over prisoners' heads; it works.

Jocelyn was marvellous and we solved the problem. If you can't see anything you're not quite sure

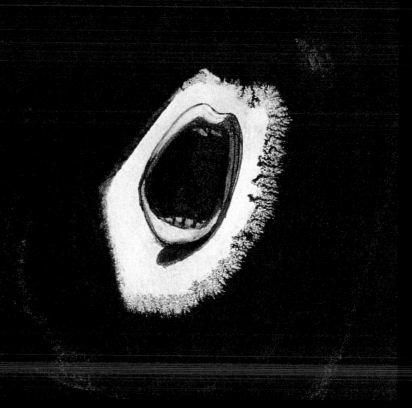

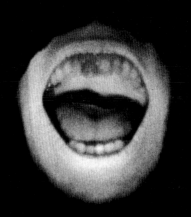

you're there, even though your brain tells you that you are. With Sam's permission we made little slits in my mask and set a little blue light at the back of the auditorium so that I knew where I was because I could always see it. Finally we did what Jocelyn had wanted to do originally, which was to strap me in a chair. My head was clamped in because otherwise I'd get the shakes and it would start to quiver. I'm very volatile and usually wave my arms like a windmill but in this play there was nowhere for that energy to go so I asked for a bar to hold onto so some of the tension could be released. A dancer has tension and then a release, tension and then a release, and acting is usually the same – after a big speech there's usually a release: in *Not I* there was no release, comfort came from nowhere.

I had a secret earpiece because I was worried about what would happen if my mind went blank. Robbie Hendry, the prompt, would know if I needed help because the rhythm would start to go and, if there was a split second pause, he'd throw me a word and I was off again. The fact that I knew that could happen gave me a feeling of comfort. Sometimes I was like a frog, I just needed a little flick to get me going again.

Every night was like falling backwards into hell, there was no way round and it was awful. I still get dizzy just remembering the play and, in fact, the tension damaged my spine and I have had to see a neurologist ever since. I call it raging Beckettitis.

Photo: John Haynes

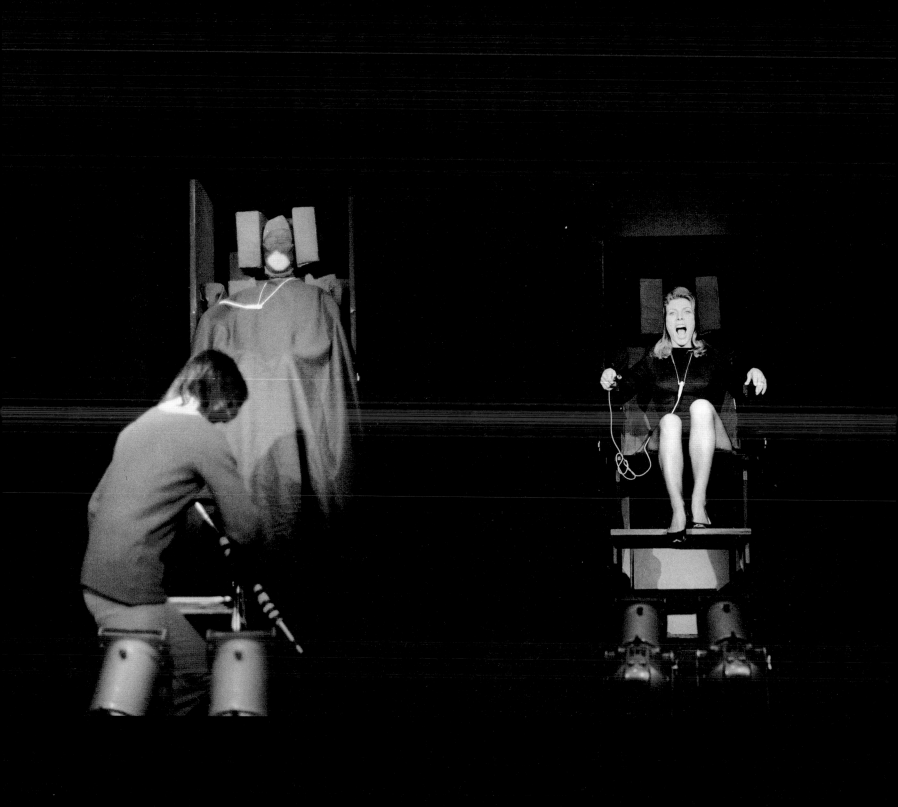

Billie Whitelaw clamped in position for Not I *and wearing the costume which blacked out all but her mouth.* **Photos: John Haynes**

Footfalls

Samuel Beckett, *Director: Samuel Beckett*
20 May 1976, The Royal Court Theatre (world première).

Footfalls *is written for the voice of an unseen actress in the upstage darkness and a figure, May, who paces back and forth across a specified area of the ground throughout the play. Beckett asks for a bare stage dimly lit with the strongest light at floor level.*

JH: In *Footfalls* the swishing noise of the figure's dress was very important so I made a taffeta petticoat. After that, I went to the Portobello Road and bought a very old lace evening dress with long sleeves and a lot of lacy net curtains which I dyed different greys and shredded. I took the sleeves off the dress and left a bit at the top to rag and gradually imposed torn bits of net in layers on top. Originally the shoes were going to be noisy but in the end we left it as just the swishing of petticoats.

When I was talking to Sam Beckett about what the character was like he kept crossing his arms over his chest and saying, "I think she'd be like this, she'd be shrinking back into herself and hiding away." He used that gesture in the production.

Below *Sketch for* Footfalls *showing the gesture Beckett made when describing the character, M. Billie Whitelaw incorporated this into her performance, moving her arms from elbow to shoulder in three stages as the play progressed.*

Below left *The figure pacing in the defined pathway of light.*

Facing page *Billie Whitelaw in performance.*
Photo: John Haynes

92

Life Class

David Storey, *Director:* Lindsay Anderson
9 April 1974, The Royal Court Theatre (world première).

The play takes place in a studio of an art school.

JH: For *Life Class* I started going to night classes at an art school in Lime Grove. (I'd been wanting to do some life drawing for a long time, something quite different from the theatre and I carried on going after the production was over.) We decided to do the play with very little scenery, it was just a room with a skylight. I'd made notes of the equipment and lights and the fires they had on stands at Lime Grove, and we were able to get hold of most of the furniture from various art schools. Finding the statue of Athene was a problem and I ended up having to get one made. In the end the cast used their own drawings and got quite keen. The beautiful forecloth of a Blake drawing was Lindsay Anderson's idea and David Lawes painted it.

David Storey: Jocelyn's set was absolutely what I had in mind and seemed totally integrated with what I'd written. I couldn't tell the difference between what I'd imagined and what we ended up with. Again, it's all down to her knack of tuning into the material which, I think, is very important to her. She needs to be not just theoretically involved but emotionally involved as well.

Jocelyn Herbert in the stalls of The Royal Court Theatre. Photo: John Haynes

The Royal National Theatre

Play

Samuel Beckett, *Director:* George Devine
7 April 1964, The National Theatre at The Old Vic (first British performance).

The play requires the three actors' heads to appear at the top of identical grey urns.

JH: The urns had to be high but not as high as the actors, who couldn't really squat because their knees would have come out too far, so I built the urns up on a platform and the cast stood below it. The urns opened at the back and could be fastened with a flap and I put foam rubber at the top with chamois over that because they had to fit as tightly as possible round the actors' shoulders. The actors were given something to hold onto during the performance. We chose dessicated wigs made as if they were the actors' own hair, but thinning and gone to seed. We made make-up out of oatmeal mixed with water and a little glue – the kind you use to stick on moustaches – and put ordinary make-up on first and then covered the actors' faces with the mixture. Lastly, we added grey and white pancake. They looked like old stone and the surface of their skin appeared to flake off during the performance. The urns were textured so that the actors seemed to be continuous with them.

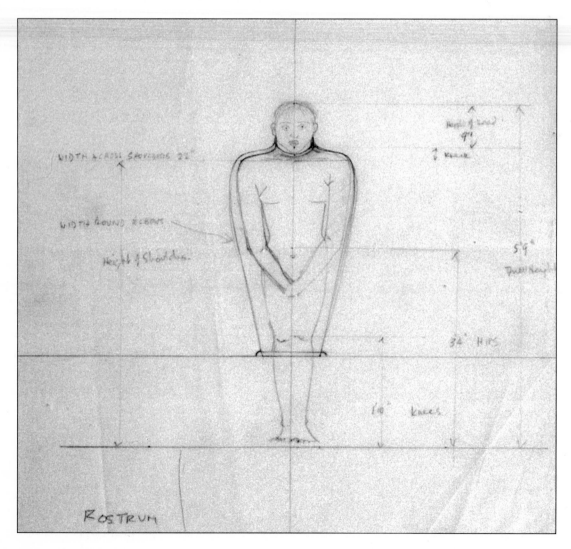

There's so little said in *Play* and yet it's the eternal triangle absolutely described. George Devine rehearsed for about two weeks with the actors in the urns to get them to know the lines so they'd be absolutely secure by the time Sam Beckett came over. At that stage they weren't speaking it fast, they were just learning the text. The characters couldn't speak unless the lamp (which was below them in the pit) was turned on them and that had to be meticulously rehearsed as well. Sam came over and they started speeding up because *Play* is supposed to be very fast. It worked perfectly because they were utterly certain of the lines.

Then George got a letter from Ken Tynan [Literary Manager of The National Theatre] saying that since Sam had arrived the whole thing had gone to pot because the actors were all gabbling and no-one could understand what they were saying. George blew up and told him to mind his own business, and then there was another letter, this time from Laurence Olivier [at that time Director of The National]. Tynan and Olivier wanted to stop Sam from going to rehearsals. George said either he would do the play as he and Sam wanted it or he wouldn't do it at all and so The National caved in. It was a tremendous success, and we revived it at The Court in 1970. This was the first time I met Billie Whitelaw and from then on it was always an immense pleasure to work with her on a play by Beckett. She seemed to have an intuitive understanding of his plays and worked closely with him in achieving a performance that he felt was right for the text.

Facing page *Plan for the urns.*
Below *The lit faces (Rosemary Harris, Robert Stephens and Billie Whitelaw).* Photo: Zoë Dominic

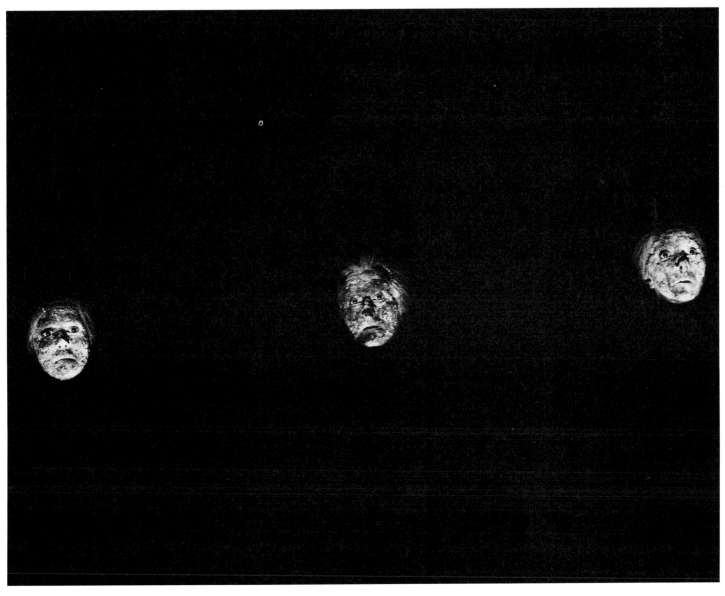

Othello

William Shakespeare, *Director:* John Dexter
21 April 1964, The National Theatre at The Old Vic.

The play demands: streets in Venice; a council chamber; Cyprus streets and a quayside; the exterior of a castle and various interior rooms, including Desdemona's bedchamber. Othello was played by Laurence Olivier.

Facing page *First costume drawing for Othello
(Laurence Olivier).*

Right *Early sketches for* Othello.

This page above and facing page *Early sketches for* Othello.

Left *Production photograph showing the doorway framed by the archway and the translucent curtain behind Desdemona's bed.*
Photo: Chris Arthur

 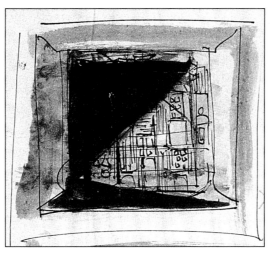 

JH: When John Dexter asked me to do *Othello* I was busy doing something else and I arrived at the design and made the model quite quickly; it was the first idea I had. John came round and loved it and, instead of going on working on it, I let it go because of the pressure of whatever else I was doing. I was always aware that I hadn't resolved all the textures and proportions and felt guilty that it could have been better.

The Old Vic had a huge forestage and doors on each side, but very little wing space. I did the Venice scenes simply by using a cut-out of the Doge's palace – a façade with triple arches – with a kind of kaleidoscope of copper and bronze behind the arches to make an interior. The exterior scene, when Brabantio is at the window, was played at night and the window was up in the side proscenium. When the action moved to the Senate the lights went up and lit the metallic collage behind the arches. I also used a curtain with the Lion of Venice on it as a wipe so that scenery could be removed behind it as it was drawn across the stage and the action was continuous. When the scene changed to Cyprus, the Doge's palace flew out and there was just an orange sky and a big tower with a huge arched entrance left on stage as the Citadel. Othello arrived from behind the Citadel and came up some steps as if he were coming from the beach into the courtyard, which had a cloth on the floor made to look like huge stone slabs. For the interior scenes the archway stayed in and we added a triple arch with purply drapes in it and a seat and cushions – it had an arab look and the colours were mostly oranges and reds with brass mouldings. In the bedroom scene an enormous doorway (with a small opening at the top to let in some light) was framed in the archway and a huge curtain came down on the other side of the stage with the bed in front of it. The curtain was slightly translucent, a mixture of solid shapes on heavy net, and there was just a single lamp hanging by the bed so that the audience could see Othello coming in while Desdemona slept.

I remember saying to John, "If we're going to do *Othello*, let's have an Othello who is proud to be black and who isn't trying to look like a Venetian." I'd looked at a lot of Delacroix's marvellous drawings of Moors and sent some to Larry Olivier to show him their hairstyles, beards and moustaches. Eventually, I did a drawing of Othello in a white robe and bare feet which both John and Larry liked. Then Peter O'Toole told Larry that if he was going to black up he ought to wear blue. I didn't like the idea of this; the colours in the design were hot colours and there was no blue in it. I'd designed some jewellery and I had it made up out of beaten metal and we went ahead and had the costume I had designed made up. When Larry came for his first fitting he tried on the white robe, was thrilled with the jewellery which went with it, and decided straight away that that was what he would wear. It was his idea to have the dagger which he used to kill himself built into the bracelet. I then discovered that he'd ordered himself a sort of negro minstrel's wig and it took quite a long time to persuade him that it wasn't right.

Sketches for Mother Courage.

Mother Courage and Her Children

Bertolt Brecht (translated by Eric Bentley. Lyrics translated by W.H. Auden), *Director:* Bill Gaskill
12 May 1965, The National Theatre at The Old Vic (first production in English).

The action of the play takes place between 1624 – 36, during the Thirty Years War. Mother Courage pulls her covered cart across Bavaria, Poland, Moravia and Italy. Brecht asks for: a country road near a town in Dalecarlia; the General's tent and his kitchen; a military camp; the exterior of an officer's tent; a badly shot-up village; the interior of a canteen tent; a high road; the exterior of a dilapidated parsonage; the exterior of a peasant's home; a peasant's home with a huge, thatched roof, backing onto a wall of rock.

Photo: Chris J. Arthur

JH: I saw the Berliner Ensemble's production of *Mother Courage* when the company came to England in 1956, and I remember saying at the time that it was one play I'd never design because nothing could be more beautiful than that production. The first act was two hours long and in German and the theatre was crammed but there were no signs of restlessness. The impact of the performance was utterly concentrated because everything the audience saw was meaningful, allowing the actors to communicate even in a foreign language. The whole of *Mother Courage* is really based on the cart, pulling it through Europe following the war. She is a scavenger, she's a survivalist, but she's also intensely human.

The props the Berliner Ensemble used had a quality of reality and truth and 'usedness' about them which wasn't just painted; it was actually worked on. Their clothes were marvellously padded, old, frayed and darned. The quality of all that was something I don't think we'd ever seen in this country at all – our sort of breakdown was usually smearing paint on or cutting Cinderella rags. It was a lesson in a kind of perfection of truth, but it wasn't naturalistic: Brecht never tried to pretend that you were not in a theatre, he always allowed the audience to see how the production was worked. I don't think I ever saw a production of Brecht's which had a lot of mechanical things going on in it. If a scene was set in Poland he just flew in a sign saying 'Poland'; when the actors pitched their camp and needed a café they just put the wagon down, put poles up and spread awnings over them. It was all so economical and brilliant.

Bill Gaskill and I set out to do *Mother Courage* differently but the organic shape of the play means that you can't do that if you want to keep to the spirit of the text so, despite myself, I got closer and closer to Brecht's production.

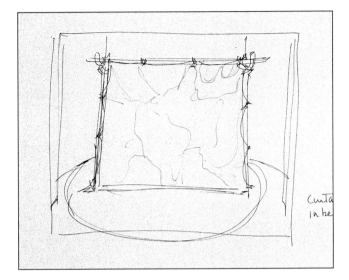

Facing page *Costume drawings for* Mother Courage.

This page top *The leather map stretched on poles.*

Right *Storyboard for* Mother Courage.

A Woman Killed With Kindness

Thomas Heywood, *Director:* John Dexter
7 April 1971, The National Theatre at The Old Vic.

First acted in 1603, the play is set inside English country houses and their grounds. Heywood's prologue speaks of a 'bare scene'.

JH: When Shakespeare was writing they had a stage and costumes and props but they didn't really have scenery, although doors were gradually introduced. I wanted to do *A Woman Killed With Kindness* in an Elizabethan way that was also right for today. I gradually evolved a set using a brown surround and a platform on two levels with walk-offs up and downstage. It was quite flexible; actors could come on at the back and from the front and go up the side.

There are a lot of servants in the play and the whole principle behind the set was to use them to move the furniture on and off to change the scenes. I made elaborate costumes and wonderful furniture and props; often just a chair or a footstool were carried on stage, but always as part of the action because it's a very flowing play. All the furniture and props were made at The National workshops with great love and skill.

I needed an overhead grid to light the play. I knew The National would say I couldn't have it because we were running in repertory, so I put the lighting-grid into the model and hung little lamps from it as if they were part of the scenery and because it was presented like that The National accepted it. *A Woman Killed With Kindness* became one of John Dexter's hallmarks. He always asks for sets like *Woman Killed*.

John Dexter: The bare stage is almost all I want to work with; a contained space in the middle of an open space. There were complaints from the critics that *A Woman Killed With Kindness* was drab: they simply didn't know what they were watching. I think it's an extraordinary, very important and moving play. *A Woman Killed With Kindness* is my favourite production of all those I've done with Jocelyn. The costumes were exquisite. It was the first time we worked with Andy Phillips, so the lighting was absolutely sympathetic to the scenery for the first time.

Facing page *Costume drawings and sketch for* A Woman Killed With Kindness.

Above *Basic set drawing for* A Woman Killed With Kindness.

RALPH RICHARDSON.   "EARLY

Early Days

David Storey, *Director:* Lindsay Anderson

31 March 1980, The National Theatre at The Theatre Royal, Brighton, transferring to The Cottesloe 22 April 1980 (world première).

Early Days *was written for Ralph Richardson (who played Kitchen) and Storey had envisaged it being done at The Royal Court Theatre. His published text doesn't specify a set.*

JH: *Early Days* is a very strange and beautiful piece and Lindsay Anderson was the perfect director for it. He and David Storey are chamber music people, and their collaborations illustrate Lindsay's sensitivity to text.

The whole idea of The Cottesloe, when the building was planned, was to have an empty room, but then they went and put galleries all round so unless you have a promenade production the sets have always to be in the same place. I put all the seats on a rake so that they confronted the actors, brought out the stage, and removed whichever parts of the galleries I could so as to make the acting area look bigger.

The set was made of three sets of gauzes, one behind the other, which had abstract trees painted on them. The idea was that Ralph Richardson would come weaving in and out through them and be picked out behind the gauze using just a little light when he first came in. Later on in the play the gauzes were lit so that they became solid. We opened in Brighton and when I arrived I found that the lights hadn't been rigged as I'd asked but instead they'd put in masses of gobos[1] to make bright orange patterns all over the set; that's what some lighting designers do. It ruined the whole mood of the design so we had to get another lighting designer to rescue us before we opened in London.

Lindsay Anderson: Jocelyn was integral to the formation of the look of *Early Days*, which affected the style of the play and how it was done. We share our values of realism derived from naturalism, but without the fussiness of naturalism, in order to achieve a poetic effect. Her set was very good, she managed to do an abstract design which both had a sense of place and also evoked the whole poetic subtext of the play which was that of memory and a certain haziness of a man not exactly in touch with concrete present circumstances. I thought it was beautifully achieved with the simplest of means.

I didn't hate The Cottesloe. Ralph was nervous of it but he acclimatised himself although he felt more at home on a proscenium stage. I think David writes in a very disciplined way in relation to the effect he wants to achieve and, therefore, a proscenium is more sympathetic to him than a space which may vary according to where you're sitting.

David Storey: I thought The Cottesloe was bloody awful. It's a young people's theatre, it has no specifics like The Court. It was just a space lit by a lamp. The exciting time was when we moved from there into The Comedy Theatre which is a little bit like The Court only grander, with the same intimacy and roughly the same shaped stage. The play suddenly became crystal clear and I felt that it was the first time I'd really seen it.

1 *Gobo: a piece of metal with a pattern cut out of it. Gobos are fitted into the lights to create shadows on the floor or backcloth and are often used to create an effect of leaves.*

Facing page *Costume drawing for Kitchen (Ralph Richardson).*

Left *Drawings for the three transparent gauzes, painted with abstract tree shapes, which were set at a distance from one another and placed with overlapping openings.*

The Life of Galileo

Bertolt Brecht (translated by Howard Brenton), *Director:* John Dexter
13 August 1980, The Olivier, The National Theatre.

The play is set in seventeenth century Italy. It calls for Galileo's studies in Padua and Florence; the Great Arsenal of Venice; the College Romanum; the vestibule of Cardinal Bellarmin's house in Rome; an ambassador's palace; a market-place; the Medici Palace in Rome; a room in the Vatican; the house where Galileo ends his days as a prisoner in Florence; a small Italian frontier town.

JH: I love The Olivier. Both John Dexter and I had been on the building committee of The National and we set out to use the space as we'd always intended it should be. Originally, it was to be built without a fly tower, but then one was added and, as a result, The Olivier mostly gets used as a proscenium theatre. This production had lots of problems and battles but it was exciting to do. Somehow I missed *Galileo* when the Berliner Ensemble brought it to London and I'd never seen it. I hoped we wouldn't do the last scene – I understand it politically but I never think it works – but in the end John Dexter included it.

I did storyboards for *Galileo*. John plans his productions minutely and likes to have little drawings to start with to help plot getting actors from one place to another and from scene to scene, and he likes to do run-throughs very quickly. That way of working comes partly from doing opera where it's

essential to plan ahead. It doesn't mean he's not flexible – if it doesn't work he'll alter it – but he has something to start with and a plan of campaign of how he will do his rehearsals. John does collaborate and, if he wants to change anything or if something isn't working well, he will always get hold of me and talk until we find another way of doing it.

For *Galileo*, John wanted as bare a stage as possible, and you need it – or the possibility of it – because of all the market scenes. One problem was how to get all the interior scenes into the open space of The Olivier stage without having a revolve, which would have been a very limiting solution. We solved it by using a truck[1] coming from the back. John was keen on the idea of projections and the metal framework around the acting area evolved because we wanted a frame for the projection screen and this then led to the decision to add the angled bits to give more shape and create entrances. I thought the play needed something metallic and technical so we made the copper astrolabe.

Facing and this page *Storyboard for* Galileo.

1 *Truck; a movable piece of scenery either on rails or wheels.*

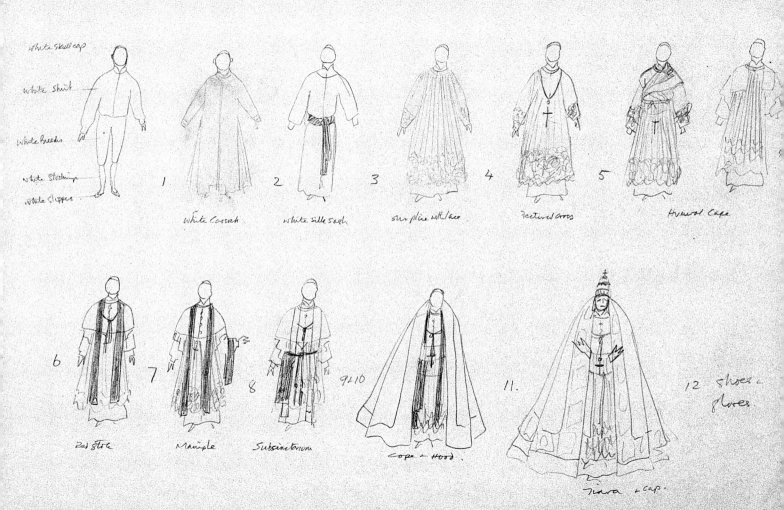

white skull cap

white Shirt

white Breeches

white Stockings

white slippers

1   white Cassock

2   white silk sash

3   surplice with lace

4   Pectoral Cross

5   Humeral Cape

6   Red Stole

7   Maniple

8   Subcinctorium

9&10   Cope + Hood.

11.   Tiara + cap.

12 shoes &
gloves.

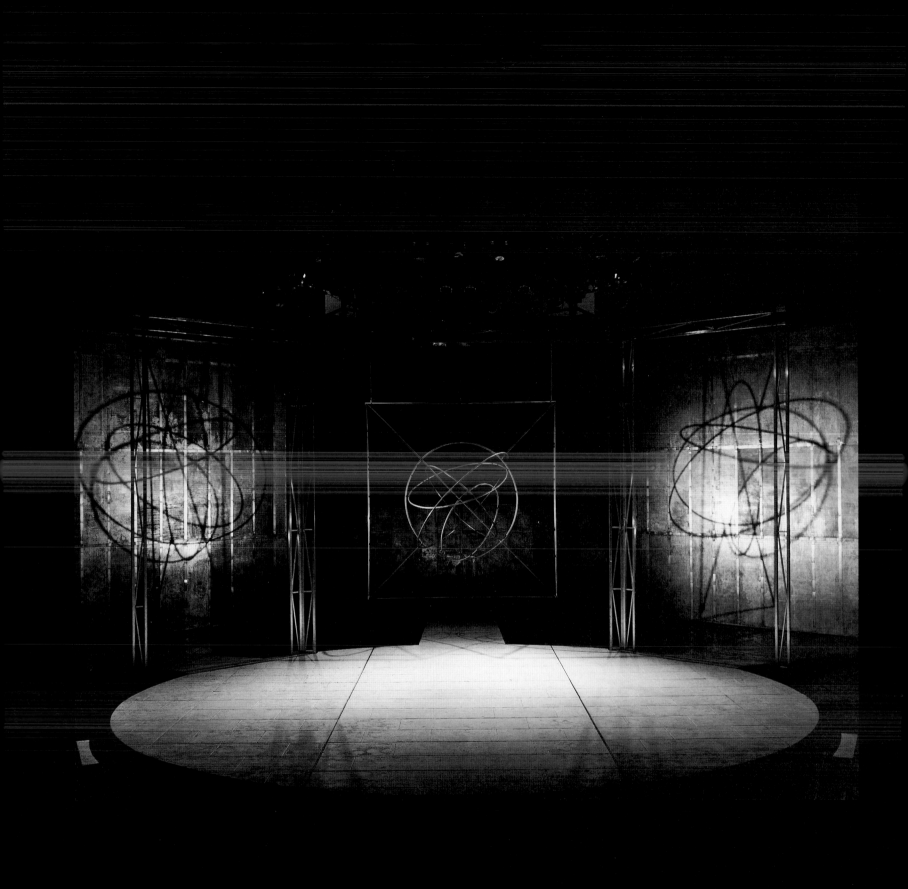

Production photographs from Galileo *showing the use of the truck.* Photos: Group Three Studio

CASSANDRA

The Oresteia

Aeschylus (translated by Tony Harrison), *Director: Peter Hall*
28 November 1981, The Olivier, The National Theatre. The production played in the amphitheatre at Epidaurus in the summer of 1982.

The Oresteia *trilogy consists of the* Agamemnon, The Choephori *and* The Eumenides. *The* Agamemnon *and* The Choephori *are set in Argos and* The Eumenides *in Delphi and Athens. The set requires the house of Atreus, the temple of Apollo and the statue of Athene. This production had a six month rehearsal period during which the masks and the costumes evolved.*

JH: The essence of Greek drama is to use the auditorium itself and just add elements where necessary. The *Agamemnon* needs a palace behind the walls of which all the terrible things happen. I wanted to use the theatre architecturally and to use the materials that The Olivier is made of. There is a series of

Facing page *Costume drawing for Cassandra.* Top *Sketch for* The Oresteia. Above *Chorus of Trojan Slave Women.*

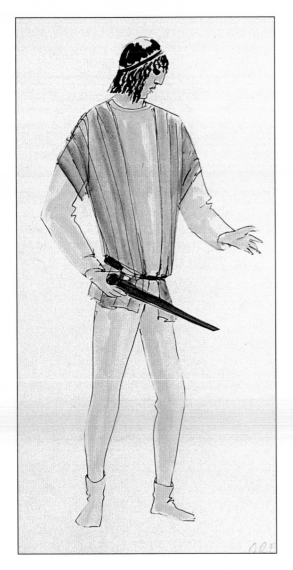

FURY

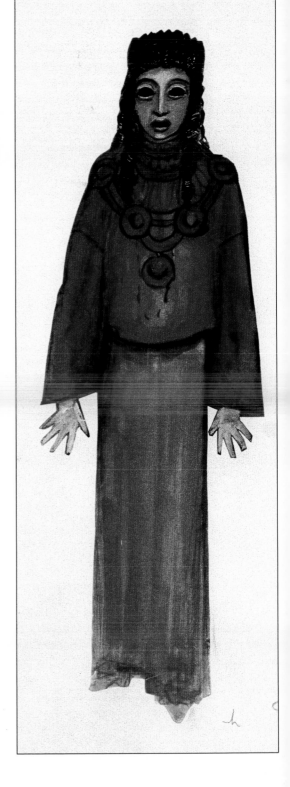

metal doors at the back of The Olivier stage which gave me the idea of making a metal façade to echo them. I designed a huge door with openings on either side, set on a raised platform with steps leading up to it. In the second act Apollo appeared in the big opening in the middle so it became his sanctuary, and in the third act the big statue of Athene was set there.

The Oresteia was the first time I'd used full-length masks and it took time to find the style and to decide whether they should be naturalistic or not. There's absolutely no tradition of masks in this country and I knew very little myself. I read a lot of Greek plays and everything that Edward Gordon Craig had written about masks. In all the Greek tragedies, none of the violence or blood-letting or agony is ever shown on stage; it all happens offstage and the audience is told about it. A mask allows the text to emerge more fully and gets rid of the very human face contortions which, quite naturally, happen when an actor describes scenes of horror.

I discovered the cast had been told it would take six months before they could utter a word and were very disturbed by the idea of masks. Before I was involved, they had been given a mixture of masks that had nothing to do with *The Oresteia* so, naturally, they couldn't speak. They had been told to look in the mirror all the time, and that is one thing you don't do with tragic masks. The tradition is that you never look in the mirror with a tragic or serious mask: the actor looks at the mask, puts it on and lets the text motivate his moves and gestures. The practice of looking in the mirror comes from the half-masks used in comedy where an actor looks at his reflection to find his character.

Facing page from left to right *Costume drawings for Orestes, a Fury, Clytemnestra.*

This page top *Chorus of Old Men (Epidaurus).*
Photo: Sue Jenkinson

Right *Drawing for Chorus of Old Men.*

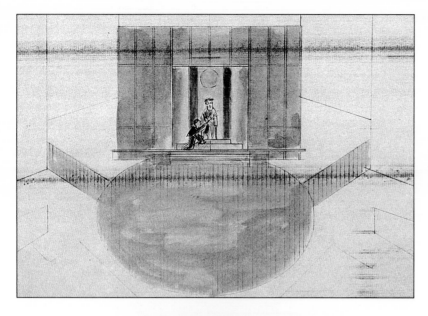

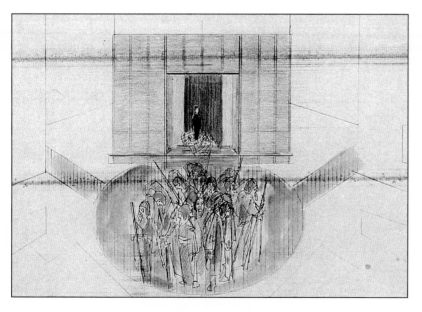

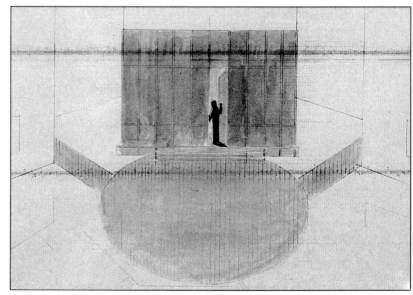

I had two assistants, Jenny West and Sue Jenkinson, to help me with the masks. To start with we made some abstract and some more real, and the actors were given them to try. We discovered that we could make shapes which looked good in clay but, by the time we'd cast them and made moulds and then the masks themselves, they sometimes didn't work at all. Understanding why some shapes don't say anything can be very confusing; one reason is that they need to be much stronger at the sculptural, clay stage than one would instinctively make them and the emphases must be moulded very boldly. The paint needs to be virtually all one colour as it is the shadows thrown by the moulding that give the character rather than the paint. We tried various materials, and would have loved to use leather but it would have taken too long to make as many masks as we needed. Fibreglass was too hard and heavy, and in the end we used four layers of muslin so the masks were light and porous. We did most of the painting and The National made the hair, which was usually black or dyed silk or cotton cord except for the Furies, for which we used dyed string.

One of the problems was that each character had to have an open mouth and that is such an expressive feature. The Furies are described as hideous figures with bloodshot eyes and snot coming out of their noses, and Peter Hall wanted bestial masks with blood coming from the mouths. The result was that the actors became like animals, tracking about, but that didn't seem to work with the text. We kept trying different faces and it was only gradually that we found it worked much better to make them rather beautiful and strange, and the text and the way the actors moved did the rest.

The masks for the Old Men of Argos were originally going to be more abstract, using a wonderful African mask as a base, but I realised it wouldn't work and that they needed to be more naturalistic. They were rather sallow and pale because of their age, with grey shadows. If you have a chorus of old men even if they're not all speaking the same lines they are in effect saying the same thing; the essence

Facing page *Storyboard for* The Oresteia.
Above *Fury in red cloak.*
Above right *Athene and Furies (Epidaurus).*
Photos: Sue Jenkinson

Left *Basic set: Metal wall, platform and steps with circular stage (Olivier).* Right *Statue of Athene in central opening (Olivier).* Photos: anon

of their characters is that they are old, life is more or less finished for them and they're always sitting waiting. If I had had sixteen different male masks it would have been very confusing but by making them similar I could enhance the telling of the story by strengthening the feeling of age, of things remembered, and of coming near the end. Somehow, although the Old Men of Argos were all in the same mask, they each looked slightly different.

Peter wanted the cast to wear clothes based on Greek costumes but which didn't look too Greek. I thought they should have costumes while we were doing the workshops and I got some cheesecloth and made some droopy garments, each with slightly different details, and told them they could choose whichever they liked and wear them in any way they wanted. I used to do little drawings of them in rehearsal and when I felt that a costume or a detail worked I fixed on that. I found some fishnet and threaded pieces of material through it and used that method for quite a lot of the costumes, especially the Furies, so that they were light and moved well. The soldiers were rather simple, based on Nazi-style black leather type of people.

When I began work on the set I didn't know that we would be playing *The Oresteia* in Greece but I'd been to Epidaurus before. For Greece I made a huge doorway and façade of what looked like the stones of Epidaurus with a curtain at the back and a platform in front with steps leading down to the ground. It was about twenty five feet high and the scale was marvellous. The lighting was much simpler and better than in London where the focusing was done without a single mask on stage. Harry Birtwistle's music sounded quite beautiful in that space. At the end the actors went right up the steps to the top of the arena leaving just the torch burning on stage; it was magical with the Furies weaving round and all the bats and moths circling in the lights.

Left top *Orestes and the Furies.* Photo: *David Hawtin*

Facing page centre *Cassandra*, clockwise from top left *Agamemnon, Aegisthus, Clytemnestra, Nurse, Electra, Chorus (Trojan Woman), Chorus (Old Man), Orestes.* Photos: *Sue Jenkinson*

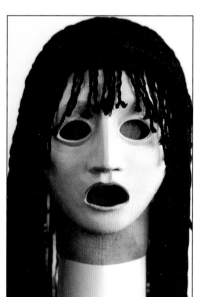

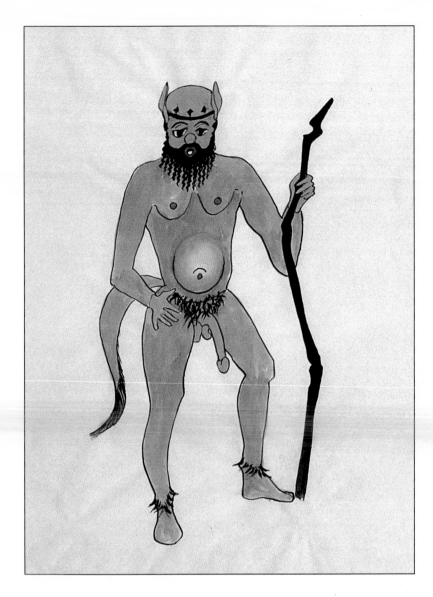

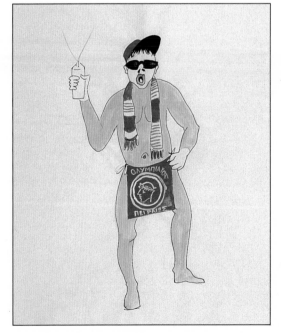

The Trackers of Oxyrhynchus

Tony Harrison, *Director:* Tony Harrison
12 July 1988, the Ancient Stadium of Delphi (world première, single performance only. The production was later re-created at The National Theatre, (Olivier)).

JH: *Trackers* is based on the remnants of a Satyr play by Sophocles which were found at Oxyrhynchus. Tony Harrison wrote it to be performed in the Stadium at Delphi for the International Theatre Festival which has been held annually for the last five years. The play had four principals and a chorus of twelve who were first satyrs and then football hooligans.

The pieces of Sophocles' text were found written on scraps of papyrus in rubbish dumps in Egypt and Tony had to track his way through them to find the play, and his feeling of tracking inspired the whole production. The Stadium is seven hundred feet long and he wanted to use as much of it as possible and wrote the play to include the echoes of the crowds at the ancient Pythian games, where the relay race of the Fellaheens was run, and also a football match for the hooligans. We divided the Stadium into three acting areas separated by tall central screens painted to look like the papyrus fragments. They were twenty feet high and stretched across the centre of the Stadium hung from wires and tied to trees on each side. The wires were attached to metal poles which gave the illusion of football goals when the screens were burnt by the hooligans, and collapsed towards the end of the play.

Trackers opened with two archeologists hunting for the papyrus in Egypt. They had large wooden crates into which they put their findings and, gradually, all the crates were assembled in a strict formation in front of the first screen. When the archeologists finally discovered the Sophocles text the Satyr play started: the first screen was lit and at a repeated call from Silenus the four sides of the crates fell open to reveal a satyr in each one. This was entirely Tony's idea and all I did was to work it out technically.

Facing page, top far left Silenus. *Left* Satyr.
Below Costume drawings for Football Hooligans.

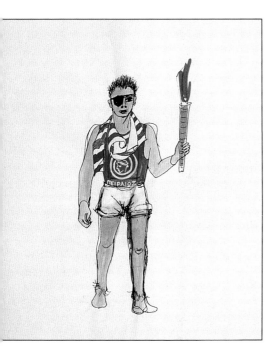

Above left *Hunt (Barrie Rutter)*. Above right *Grenfell (Jack Shepherd)*. Facing page *Costume drawings for Egyptian workers (the Fellaheens)*.

Fellaheen

Facing page *The set, with the packing cases open to create the 'floor'.*
Photo: Vicki Hallam

Top *Kyllene (Juliet Stevenson).*
Photo: Sandra Lousada

Top right *Jocelyn Herbert at work in Delphi.*
Photo: Max Harrison

Right *The Satyrs.*
Photo: Sandra Lousada

Square Rounds

Tony Harrison, *Director:* Tony Harrison
1 October 1992, The Olivier, The Royal National Theatre (world *première*).

JH: The writing of this play was a voyage of discovery for everyone involved. We had an early explorative workshop where it became obvious that music, singing, movement and also magic and conjuring were all essential elements in illuminating the text. Tony Harrison decided to go ahead and went away to write. I made a rough model in preparation for the second workshop some months later, when Tony had some more text to work on. As a result of this workshop Tony decided to have an all women cast, the argument being that as it was 1914 and women were for the first time doing men's jobs in munitions factories etc., why shouldn't they also do actors' jobs and play men's parts in the theatre?

The main visual element that obsessed Tony was the black top hat. It was the symbol of the black frock-coated scientists of the early twentieth century and the same formal attire was still worn by many conjurors and magicians today. So the basis of the design, it seemed, had to be black and white. I covered the entire Olivier stage with white flooring, and the three back shutters with white projection cloth framed by black velvet. On these we projected pictures of a devastated war landscape with scarred and mangled trees. We decided to use the rim revolve, which was covered with black carpet, so giving us a white floor with a circular moving track two metres wide, its radius being the centre of the stage. I flew a large flat covered with black velvet into the white centre which, with the black circle, gave the impression of an enormous top hat. This flat could fly in and out when needed, revealing what or who had been set behind it. Actors came up from below stage through traps so that their entrances were, we hoped, not seen by the audience. The few scenic elements needed for the different scenes also appeared in this way to avoid scene change hold-ups.

To give an insight into the heart of this enormously courageous and inventive work, there is a verse sung by Hiram Maxim (the inventor of the machine gun) after his horror on discovering that a chemist had developed poison gas as a means of killing men:

> *"Nitrates we saw for Peace and for War*
> *Black's always there with the white,*
> *One good, one bad force, from the very same source*
> *The darkness contained in the light."*

The contrast throughout the play of the duality of beauty and destruction – chemicals making coloured dyes but also poisoned gas, nitrates as fertilizers and also T.N.T., gunpowder sometimes making weapons, sometimes fireworks – was illustrated by many magical happenings and conjuring tricks seeming to come from normal acting.

Tony had discovered that China, 2,000 years ago, had all the terrible weapons we have today but made out of bamboo and human shit. Again, bamboo could be turned into a gun or a flute. After the discovery and subsequent use of poison gas and the flying in of brilliantly coloured silk gas clouds, the last part of the play gradually changed to China. The end was an explosion of colour demonstrated by the cast, now dressed as colourful Chinese, and their singing and dancing (Chinese style) until they in their turn disappeared leaving the vision of the horrors of 1992. Finally, the audience was left with the bare stage we had started with.

Production photograph showing the gas-masks and the
coloured scarves used to represent the poison gas.
Photo: Nobby Clark

Above *Tony Harrison at work on Square Rounds.*

Top *The empty set for* Square Rounds. **Middle** *Photograph of the model for* Square Rounds *(Chinese Scene). The coloured clouds represented the different gases.* **Above** *Tony Harrison and Jocelyn Herbert during work on* Square Rounds.

Top *The Munitionettes.* Middle *Maria Friedman (Clara Haber) and Sara Kestelman (Fritz Haber).* Above *The set showing projections in use.* Photos: Nobby Clark

Above *Production photograph showing the projections in use, the chorus and Maria Friedman (Clara Haber).*

Left *The Chinese scene.*
Photos: Nobby Clark

Stages

David Storey, *Director:* Lindsay Anderson
18 November 1992, The Cottesloe, The Royal National Theatre (world première). Alan Bates played Fenchurch in this production.

JH: The set for *Stages* evolved from the need of a double room, an archway, a window upstage and an unseen front door. It was more a dramatic poem than a normal play, and too much naturalism seemed to fight the quality of the writing. I felt the set needed to be as anonymous as possible and a very light construction, so I used metal framed flats covered with fine hessian backed with gauze, and I covered the floor with stage cloth of the same colour as the hessian. They were all painted and textured to achieve the right overall colour, which seemed to provide a place that was real and not real. Lindsay Anderson had asked for quite a lot of furniture but we soon found after the first rehearsals that it was not needed and ended up with two chairs and a bookcase downstage and a table and two chairs upstage in front of the window. The gauze windows could be lit in such a way that you could see the actors coming in through the front door and into the sitting-room and then the gauze became solid again. We did a bit of expressionistic lighting at the end when Alan Bates (Fenchurch) seemed to go mad, ending in a chaotic dance.

Lindsay Anderson: *Stages* might seem to call for a simple set. But, as so often with Storey, the text called for decor and costumes that would evoke the poetic essence of the play as well as its apparent naturalism. That is why Jocelyn's set, part real, part the stuff of imagination, worked so well in its Magritte-like way to complement the style of the writing.

Sketch for Stages.

Facing page *Sketches for* Stages.

Right *Production photograph of Alan Bates (Fenchurch).*
Photo: John Haynes

David Storey: The script of *Stages* had no stage description. What set there was had to be designed from the action and, as with previous productions (where there was more authorial assistance), Jocelyn produced something so close to the mind's eye invention of the author that it was as if she had composed the play herself – a space, in this instance, both real and abstracted, an echo of (and foil to) the elliptical and idiosyncratic mental wanderings of the central character in his confrontation with the principal female presences in his life. Her design was in a direct line of development from those of *Home* and *Early Days* – a visual suffusion of the inner and outer worlds of a character who, ostensibly, was at the end of his tether. Uniquely, none of Jocelyn's designs has ever varied from the one imagined at the time of writing – a graphic endorsement of that most mysterious and rewarding of artistic experiences – collaboration.

Jocelyn Herbert in her studio. Photo: *Julian Herbert*

Other Theatres

Richard III
under tunic

Christopher Plummer

Richard III

William Shakespeare, *Director:* Bill Gaskill
24 May 1961, The Royal Shakespeare Theatre, Stratford-upon-Avon.

*The play demands: London streets; the royal palace; the interior and walls of the
Tower of London; Pomfret Castle; the court of Baynard's Castle; open ground at Salisbury;
Bosworth Field.*

JH: I had been working mostly at The Royal Court and it was an adventure to design at Stratford. It was the first big theatre I'd worked in, and it was a bit frightening because I was doing things which nobody else had done at the time. Bill Gaskill and I were taking what we believed in at The Court to Stratford and, maybe it would have happened anyway, but *Richard III* did start off a completely new attitude to decor there. It was a time when Leslie Hurry was in full flood with his brilliant, painted sets. I had digs near to the Dirty Duck pub and used to go in for a drink on the way home and Leslie was often there. One day we found ourselves standing at the bar next to each other so I said, "I don't think anyone is ever going to introduce us because they imagine we'll bite each other's heads off," and we became great friends after that.

I wanted to do something very simple using metal as a key for the production with a plain, board floor on a rake. The model consisted of a wooden floor with a tower covered in different gauzes, a metal surround and metal shields flying in. There was very little on stage most of the time but then Bill got obsessed about needing a door for Hastings to come and knock on and it took a long time to get him off that. We had a problem with the tents in Act 3; Bill wanted real tents so I did various designs and made some up but they looked wrong. Then he came up with the idea of using the soldiers in huge cloaks to stand round with their backs turned to form the tents and that worked perfectly.

Facing page *Costume drawing for Richard III
(Christopher Plummer).*

Right *The Mourners.*

Although I'd used metal in *Antigone* in 1960 at The Court, it was *Richard III* that brought it into use with a bang. It was quite a breakthrough. The workshops were very reluctant to use it and kept insisting that they could paint wood to look like metal. They kept on saying, "You've only designed in a small theatre, you don't understand." The man whose job it was to paint the scenery wanted to paint the floor but I insisted that I just wanted dirty water thrown over it.

I had a big metal grille at the back, made from the thin strips of the mesh that you put round building sites, and behind that was a cloth. The backcloth could be lit so that the grille was invisible for scenes that needed a sense of distance and, when a hard scene was playing, it could be lit so that the bars of the grid were picked out and it became more sinister. Again, the workshop wanted to paint the grid on the backcloth and I had to fight that. There were terrific difficulties about the lighting and the Stratford people couldn't do what we asked for, so Richard Pilbrow came and took over and was able to give us everything we'd wanted after all.

There was a great battle because the materials for the costumes were supposed to be dyed and painted before they were cut; the painters had nothing to do and the dyer was overworked but the painters weren't allowed to help out because it wasn't strictly their job. I had thought that, after The Court, working at Stratford would mean that everything would be done for me, but I still ended up working all night.

Facing page and this page *Costume drawings for* Richard III.

Left *Production photograph of Christopher Plummer as Richard III, showing the tower and the sun emblem.*

Right *Production photograph of Richard III showing the bare boards of the stage. Christopher Plummer (Richard III) with Edith Evans (Queen Margaret) and Eric Porter (Buckingham).*   Photos: Angus McBean

Baal

Bertolt Brecht, *Director:* Bill Gaskill

7 February 1963, The Phoenix Theatre (world première).

The playwright asks for: a dining room; Baal's attic; an inn; whitewashed houses with brown tree trunks; night beneath the trees; a club called 'The Night Cloud'; green fields; blue plum trees; a village inn; trees in the evening; a hut; a plain; sky; a brown wooden bar; green thicket; river beyond; a country road; willows; young hazel shrubs; a maple tree in the wind; 10 E of Greenwich; forest; a country road; a hut in the forest.

First sketches for Baal.

JH: *Baal* had never been done and there was nothing written about it anywhere, so in a sense we were quite free. There's a strangeness about the text, which has savagery and poetry at the same time; lots of moments in the play are very alienating and then someone will suddenly go into song. I'm sure Brecht would have done it more savagely, and I think the criticism of our production was that Peter O'Toole [Baal] was too romantic and not uncouth enough; he didn't like being unpleasant. It may have been a bit my fault because, however seedy it was, it did actually look rather beautiful.

The sets were evocative and poetic, inspired by the few words Brecht wrote at the beginning of each scene. Extremely simple images came up on stage and, just because of their size and scale, they evoked something very beautiful. We had a huge, forty foot cyc and I used projections made from drawings with strong contrasts intensified by using grease, paint and chalk. It was a very Brechtian production and we flew in little bits of scenery and flats as we needed them.

Helie Weigel [Brecht's widow, who had played most of the leading female roles in his plays at the Berliner Ensemble] came over because she had never seen *Baal* performed and she was obviously very moved by it. I think it related to her early days with Brecht. The projections I'd used were enormous and we'd managed to get perfect joins; Helie was very interested in that and I later sent her instructions about how to do it on that scale. I was terribly overawed by her presence, but after that she was always very helpful to me.

Different plays make me draw in a different way, and I think I get influenced by the sort of books I look at when I research the background or the period. The drawings I did for *Baal* are almost caricatures, they're more violent than most of my drawings.

Facing page and this page *First sketches for* Baal.

151

Costume drawings for Baal.

Production photographs for Baal. *Photos: Lewis Morley*

Pygmalion

George Bernard Shaw, *Director:* John Dexter
16 May 1974, The Albery Theatre.

The production required: the portico of St. Paul's church in Covent Garden vegetable market; Henry Higgins' laboratory in Wimpole Street containing a fireplace, a leather easy-chair, three further chairs, a stand for newspapers, a grand piano, filing cabinets, a writing table, a phonograph, a laryngoscope, a row of tiny organ pipes with bellows, a set of lamp chimneys for singing flames, a lifesize image of half a human head; Mrs Higgins' drawing room in a flat on the Chelsea Embankment, a room whose decor shows the influence of William Morris and Burne-Jones and for which Shaw specifies a big Ottoman, a Chippendale chair, an Elizabethan chair "in the taste of Inigo Jones", a piano, a fireplace and a divan as well as oil paintings and three windows overlooking the river.

JH: Period plays like *Pygmalion* are a bit of a challenge, and this was the first production of that nature I'd done. It was immensely elaborate compared to doing Shakespeare where you can get away with having very little, but the richness and clutter is very much part of Shaw's work. His plays, like Chekhov's, are of a certain historical time and don't make sense if you try to stage them in another period.

Above *Diana Rigg as Eliza.*
Photo: Zoë Dominic

Right *First scribbles for Pygmalion.*

John Dexter wanted to go from scene to scene without a break so we decided to use a revolve. Revolves are a bit maddening; you make the set for the next scene on the back of the one before it, but however differently you think you've done each of them, you tend to find you've made the same kind of space because each one is wedge-shaped. The set was surrounded by blacks with a black floor, and only the revolve was lit.

I made the portico of St. Paul's church using a pillar (which was trucked out at the end of the scene) and a flat. The important element is the lamp and I based mine on a real one outside the church. Higgins' room was set behind St. Paul's on the revolve and was very masculine, with a huge fireplace, leather chairs and all his machinery; it was utterly naturalistic, but it wasn't complete or real in the way that a box set attempts because, for instance, there were only two walls. Mrs Higgins' house was Edwardian with very heavy mouldings, and I drew on memories of a house I used to visit as a child that belonged to the woman reputed to have been Rossetti's last love. I chose a William Morris style flowery wallpaper and a lamp with an herbaceous border cut in iron – she had pictures everywhere and even the piano was decorated.

You have to respect Shaw's stage directions. John, for some reason, wanted to put the fireplace on the other side of the room in Mrs Higgins' house. I couldn't make it work because I hadn't got a wall on that side so I promised to try a free-standing fireplace. Before I had time to work on it he rang to say not to worry because later on Higgins has to fall over the coal-scuttle and the scene couldn't work if the fireplace wasn't where Shaw asked it to be. The only way you could alter the placing of the fireplace was to reverse the whole set.

Facing page bottom *Covent Garden.* Above *Costume drawing for Eliza (Diana Rigg) as a flowergirl.* This page above left *Costume drawing and fabric samples for Higgins (Alec McCowen).* Above right *Costume drawing for Eliza in Act 4.*

The Portage to San Cristobal of A.H.

George Steiner, adapted by Christopher Hampton, *Director:* John Dexter
17 February 1982, The Mermaid Theatre (world première).

The play is set in May 1979 in a remote area of Brazil, and in Oxford, Moscow, Cologne, Paris and Washington.

JH: The Mermaid is a very intimate theatre and I love the confrontation of the stage and the straight down rake of the seats. I always hoped The Lyttelton would be like that, but there they made the mistake of putting in the gallery. The real problem with The Mermaid stage is that it is immensely deep and the proportions are, therefore, wrong. All the rebuilding money seems to have been spent on the restaurant and bars and on beautiful parquet floors in the rehearsal rooms. You can only enter the stage from one side and if you need a downstage entrance it has to be masked, which is a pity and it means that you have to put something across the back so that people can get backstage by walking upstage behind it. I got the idea for a scaffolding bridge downstage and the interiors came in on a truck from the back.

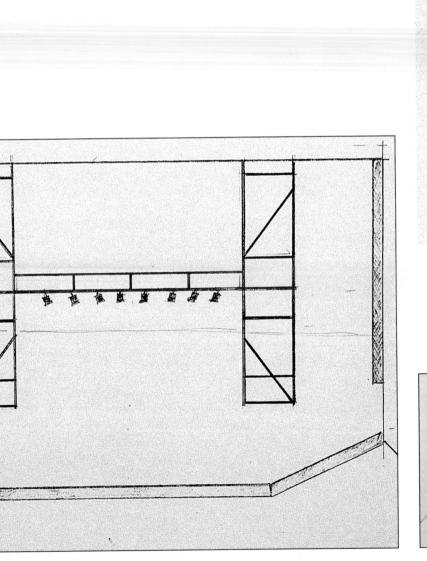

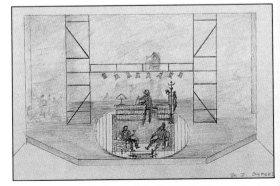

158

Facing page bottom *Set drawings.*

Above *Costume drawing for A.H. (Alec McCowen).*

Right *Storyboard for* The Portage to San Cristobal of A.H.

ELLIE ACT I

HESIONE ACT I

Above *Set drawing for* Heartbreak House.

Far left, left and facing page middle and far right *Costume drawings for* Heartbreak House.

Facing page top *Photograph of Rex Harrison in the final costume.*
Photo: Zoë Dominic

Right *Drawing showing the clothes Rex Harrison (Captain Shotover) asked for at the beginning of rehearsals.*

Heartbreak House

George Bernard Shaw, *Director: John Dexter*
10 March 1983, The Haymarket Theatre.

The play opens in a room built to resemble "the afterpart of an old-fashioned, high-pooped ship with a stern gallery" (which Shaw describes in detail), through the windows of which can be seen the hilly countryside of the north edge of Sussex. The last act takes place on a terrace beside the house and Shaw asks for a flagstaff, a hammock, a garden seat and a deckchair. Rex Harrison played Captain Shotover in this production.

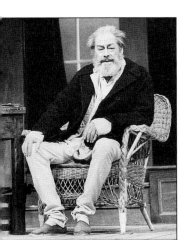

JH: This is a difficult set to do because so much is asked for and, although I achieved the feeling of a ship, I may have simplified too much – it didn't have the usual Shavian opulence and clutter.

I had problems with Rex Harrison's costume in *Heartbreak House*. He wanted to wear the proper reefer jacket from Watts, the yachting place, and a navy blue sweater and black boots. I thought it was completely wrong, but I got him what he asked for. I also got a very old donkey jacket from Portobello Road, and I made some old dhotis – those baggy Indian trousers made of cheesecloth – and collected an Indian-type shirt and waistcoat, an old cap and some espadrilles.

Time passed and he didn't seem to be getting the part and John Dexter was in despair. We tried different coats, all of the same kind Rex had asked for. One day he said he didn't know about the costume, that it didn't seem to give him anything. I suggested he tried the old clothes I'd collected. He put them on and suddenly saw how he could play the part. The trousers were shapeless and hung on him – I explained they were things he had picked up on his travels, and that he didn't mind any more about clothes, it was part of his eccentricity. I put the espadrilles out and he was very suspicious of those but they helped him to shuffle about like an old man. From the moment he put the costume on his performance took off and it was fascinating to watch it develop. The old clothes gave Rex a way of doing the part; you can't impose that sort of thing, you just have to wait for it to happen.

The Devil and the Good Lord

Jean-Paul Sartre (translated by Frank Hauser), *Director:* John Dexter
6 September 1984, The Lyric Theatre, Hammersmith.

The play is set in Germany in 1524 "between heaven and earth" and requires: a hall in the Archbishop's palace and the ramparts of the town of Worms; the outskirts of Goetz's camp with the town in the background; the castle of Heidenstamm; before the portal of a village church; the interior of the church; a square in Altweiler; the peasants' camp; the ruined village.

JH: For *The Devil and the Good Lord* I used a black surround and a platform on a boarded floor with steps leading up to it. The play has about twenty five scenes and it is set way back in the period past. To try to show all those different places was, to me, impossible without ruining the production because, even if we had had the money, it would have had to be such a heavy business. The moment I put anything real in the set it would have been in the way of the next scene so I felt everything that went on stage had to be abstract, like a painting.

Left *Sketch for Church Act 2, Sc 3.*

Facing page *Production photograph of Gerard Murphy (Goetz) showing use of the crates.*
Photo: Donald Cooper

I hit on the idea that crates could be used by the actors to build whatever was needed, for instance a window or a pulpit, by piling them on top of one another in different ways. I knew using crates would interest John Dexter. It was like *Chips With Everything*, as soon as he had caught onto the idea he used it brilliantly. *The Devil and the Good Lord* set was like a Ben Nicholson painting, architectural shapes which were timeless and purely formal in quality. The only things we flew in were a bit of tent and the crucifix. The carving of the Christ was based on the Grünewald Crucifixion and was vast.

John wanted projections of period paintings and asked for a screen, but I couldn't make that work. I realised I could use a tall flat instead of a screen and project onto it, and that it would also give the actors an entrance at the back; I then had to balance it with a shape on the other side of the stage. I go on experimenting with a design until something happens and I find that the proportions are right and the whole thing suddenly gels. I don't consciously work it out in my head, although I may be worrying about it subconsciously, so I try all sorts of different things and suddenly recognise what I'm aiming at and see that it's going to work. I got very excited about the flat in *The Devil and the Good Lord* because I thought it gave a wonderful strength to the whole space and I kept it even though we didn't use projections in the end.

This was probably the most rigorous set I've done and the props had to be very clear and simple in their impact. Over the years I've tried to do several plays using the idea of a basic costume and I think the ones I did for *The Devil and the Good Lord* were the best resolved of that nature because I was really consistent. It's also the most economical approach because if you have one basic costume it's fairly anonymous and you can really pick out the details of the different characters very well. I had a lot of material dyed in various tones of grey, so there would be a slight variation but not much. The peasants had trousers rather like dhotis and a mixture of shirts and jackets, some with waistcoats, some without. The bourgeois barons had extras like hats, tabards and swords and the soldiers had military details added.

John Dexter: I said that the only difference I wanted from *A Woman Killed With Kindness* was that we should use building planks and make it very rough looking. I didn't envisage the crucifix being vast, that was Jocelyn. I nominate the space and Jocelyn supplies the object in space which tells you what you need to know about the scene. *The Devil and the Good Lord* looked wonderful. It's obscene what is being spent on scenery at the moment, but this production cost only about £4,000.

Left *Goetz's tent showing use of crates.* Photo: Donald Cooper

Facing page *Sketches showing variations of the basic costume for* The Devil and the Good Lord.

Gigi

Alan Jay Lerner & Frederick Loewe, *Director:* John Dexter
17 September 1985, The Lyric, Shaftesbury Avenue.

The production demanded: a bare theatre; a Catalan restaurant; Mamita's apartment; a street; Aunt Alicia's apartment; Maxim's restaurant; Honore's apartment; The Grand Hotel, Trouville; Maître du Fresne's office.

JH: *Gigi* was the first musical I'd done. There are an awful lot of scenes, some big and some intimate, and it was quite elaborate and difficult to do. John Dexter didn't want to do a large-scale musical and we thought of it more as a play with music. He had the idea that the actors should walk from one scene into another so we used a revolve, which meant we had to be very organised and make sure all the elements were flown out before it could turn.

The elements I used to create the different settings were quite small although they created a strong atmosphere. For example, I used three flats – fragments of flats rather than whole flats – as a frame for Mamita's apartment and the rest was achieved by using just furniture.

The hotel scene had a single white cut-out and a painted beach scene beyond and the rest of it was made using trees, palms and furniture.

The curtain was taken from photographs of people in the Bois du Boulogne in Paris. It curved out which meant that we could bring the revolve down as near to the curtain as possible and the set could be changed behind it, whereas if it had gone straight across it would have cut along the revolve.

Facing page *Photographs of the model for Gigi showing the different scenes.* Photos: David Crosswaite

Below left *Drawing for the front-curtain.*

Below *Maxim's.*

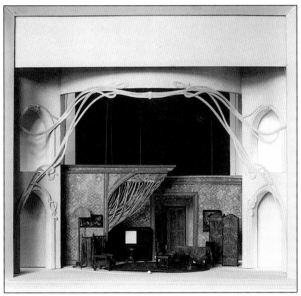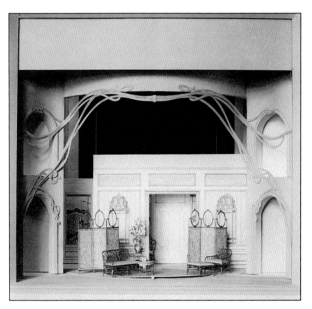

Costume drawings for Gigi.

Timon of Athens

William Shakespeare, *Director:* Simon Usher
16 February 1988, The Haymarket Theatre (studio), Leicester.

The text asks for: Timon's house in Athens; a room in a Senator's house; a room in Lucullus'
house; a public place; a room in Sempronius' house; the Senate-House; outside the walls of Athens;
woods and a cave near the sea-shore. In the Leicester studio production the play was divided into
two acts.

JH: There was a very small budget for *Timon* and only enough money to pay seven actors. For the
banquet scene we had only three people so the idea of having a great table groaning with food was
ridiculous. Simon Usher is very sensitive and intelligent and was absorbed by the text. We had several
meetings and talked about different ways of doing the play but weren't really getting anywhere. Then
he had the idea of using three of the actors like a chorus so that they would be the servants not only of
Timon but of the other characters as well. I thought that was the right way to begin thinking about it.

The set started when Simon said something about doorways and I cut out some door-frames and
worked from there. Originally there were three architraves on a swivel, but there was talk of the
production going on tour so I made them free-standing which is why they became doubled in an 'L'
shape. The centre of each one was pivoted so that they could turn and be rearranged in different
permutations. The Leicester studio is painted black and angled, and there's a floor without a stage

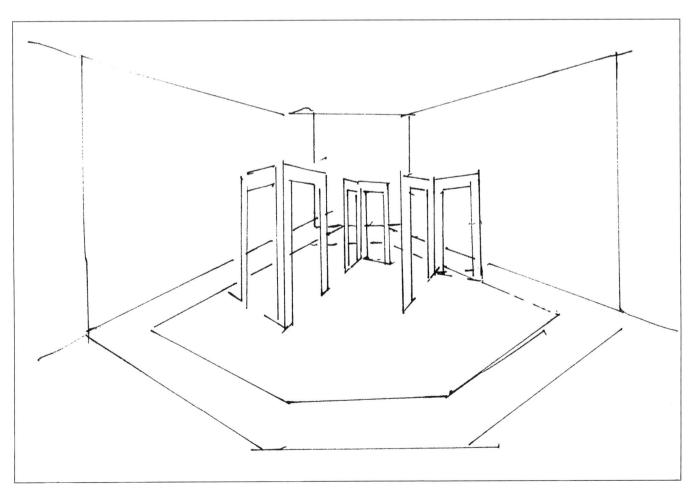

Early sketch for Timon *set.*

and three blocks of seats. The lighting-grid is only about sixteen feet above the ground, which is rather low and makes it difficult to light as precisely as one would like to. In order to make the playing area seem as big as possible we used a smaller floor area than the full studio space and made the doorways as tall as we could. I made the floor using big squares of hardboard on top of plywood. Both the floor and the doorways were mottled grey and the furniture (tables and stools) was made with grey metal legs and grey tops, so the whole set was completely grey within a black space.

Simon was able to use the door-frames to give the impression of lots of movement and people coming in one door and going out of another. We did the banquet scene as a sort of vignette, spotlit right at the back. We had a big boar's head and some wine for the first banquet and some silver lids for the second, but no more than that, because a lot of props would have been outside the rhythm and style of the production.

During the interval the doorways were moved closer together so that the light through them created the feeling of trees and Timon's cave. I laid some big stone slabs on the other side of the stage, slightly rougher in texture than the floor, and built them into a stone pyre behind which Timon could grabble for the gold. We even cut the spade we'd originally given Timon because it became unnecessary. I'm sure a lot of people thought the design too austere, but it became a good, consistent style and made it possible to do the play with such a small cast.

I found lots of costume bits in The Haymarket's store and adapted and dyed those. Because of the simplicity and abstraction of the set I thought it was better to put the play into modern dress. Simon and I discussed having a timeless ethnic sort of trousers and top, but finally decided on grey suits, which made a comment on a rather cold, gloomy, money-making society which was also appropriate for England today. I bought four grey suits, and dressed the cynic, Apemantus, in black and Alcibiades as a soldier. The suits worked with the small cast; when the noblemen became servants they just took off their jackets and wore waistcoats and ties; when the actors became Senators they slipped black robes over the top of the suits and wore hats. I found some white and grey silky material in Leicester market and made ponchos for the banquet scene to make it a bit more festive. Originally there were going to be more costume changes but we took them out because they became intrusive. For the second act, when Timon is all raggedy, we just broke down an old pair of trousers and tore up an old sweater and built his costume from there.

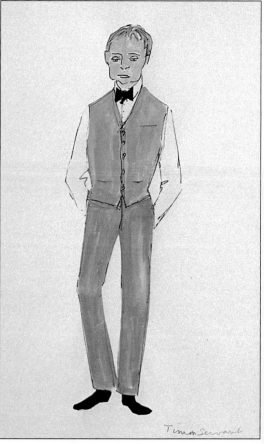

Top row from left to right *Basic grey suit; suit adapted for a Senator; adapted for a banquet guest; adapted for a gangster.*

Bottom row *Suit adapted for a waiter. Costume drawings for Soldier; Alcibiades; Apemantus.*

171

Jocelyn Herbert painting the Satyrs' boxes at Salts's Mill, Saltaire, Yorkshire.
Photo: Nobby Clark

Opera

Designing opera came quite out of the blue. As a child I learned the piano and there was always music in our home, but I'm not particularly knowledgeable about it. My mother used to take me to Covent Garden and I remember sitting through *The Ring* and feeling guilty because I couldn't find it all wonderful although there were moments that I loved. I enjoyed opera the most when I was a student in Vienna just before the war and I used to buy a ticket for a shilling and go up in the gallery. I never saw the operas at all, I used to sit with my back against the barrier and just listen.

Opera is supposed to be an extension of theatre but I don't think it works in quite that way because singers really do need to sing rather than act. A large part of the director's job in opera is to get the principals and the chorus into positions where they can see the conductor and where their voices relate to one another. It's a very intricate juggling act. Contemporary opera is much closer to theatre and demands acting as well as singing from the performers.

Orpheus and Euridice

Gluck (libretto by Calzabigi), *Director:* Glen Byam Shaw
4 October 1967, Sadler's Wells Theatre.

The opera requires: the tomb of Euridice; the Netherworld; the Elysian Fields; a forest.

Below *Costume drawing for the male chorus Act 1.*
Below right *Drawing for the chorus Act 1.*

JH: Glen Byam Shaw asked me to do *Orpheus and Euridice* and I agreed as long as we didn't do it in an eighteenth century naturalistic kind of way. Orpheus is traditionally sung by a woman, but Glen decided to have a man play it, I suppose because he thought that would be more romantic. I played and played the music and that gave me the emotion and feel for each scene. Apart from the overture and the boring eighteenth century ballet music at the end, it is such beautiful music and it's emotional in a way that hadn't been heard much before it was written. It's the music as much as the story of an opera which gives the style for the design.

I thought we should finish the opera with Orpheus' song after the death of Euridice because the music after that is of such a completely different quality, but in the end we had to do about ten minutes of the ballet music as well. The question of a choreographer came up and I was asked if I had any ideas and suggested Merce Cunningham but the Board were too alarmed even to consider him. When it came to rehearsals the choreographer wanted to have masses of dancers in the Happy Spirits scene whereas I just wanted two or three standing with white masks so that they appeared to be disembodied and moved as though blown by a gentle whiff of wind. The choreographer said he had put so many dancers in because he had to give the ballet something to do. That problem crops up in many operas when the chorus demanded is quite small but the chorus master will insist on putting the whole company on because he wants to give them work even if it ruins the scene dramatically. That was one of the rows we had at the Met in New York where they're not used to designers having feelings about these things at all.

It's quite a problem to get a chorus of eighty people on and off stage in two minutes, so you have to work very closely with the director. (For operas where it's not an integral part of the action, I'd like to build a theatre where the chorus could be in the pit.) Another difficulty that has to be solved with a

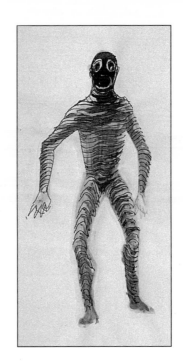

big chorus is for them all to be able to see the conductor, and I evolved a structure with a circle at the centre surrounded by a sloping ramp which enabled them to come in at the back and stand round.

The tomb was a very simple abstract shape and the set was black, white and grey with no olive trees or other naturalistic details. I had a great black sun for the first scene, which changed to gold for the ending. After the first scene, the tomb was struck leaving the circle and the walkdown.

The circle created a sense of depth for Hell – you need to find some height for the Underworld to evoke the feeling that the souls are trying to climb out. The Damned Spirits in Hell were figures wearing huge masks and dressed to look like bits of lichen. Large, abstract shapes flew in, the same kind of texture as the costumes, and the ballet of Spirits was in the centre circle, writhing as if they were caught in mud. Orpheus entered through flames, which we achieved using lights.

The set worked marvellously for the Happy Spirits scene because we turned the circle into a pool just by putting a blue light on it. That scene is supposed to be very empty with just the heavenly voices and I managed, after a great battle, to have the chorus placed behind the backcloth.

The costumes were perhaps too Greek. I think the very simple mourning drapes worked for the chorus, but I wasn't happy with the principals' costumes. For the end we painted all the materials with patterns, which looked lovely, but I don't feel I resolved the costumes properly, something didn't quite work and they weren't in the same style as the set.

The design for this did strike a great blow because it was very abstract for that time. Glen Byam Shaw was not an adventurous director from the design point of view but he loved this set. I was teaching at Percy Harris' school so the students came to rehearsals and I think the production had quite a lot of influence on them.

Margaret [Percy] Harris: I was the Resident Designer at Sadler's Wells at the time Jocelyn did *Orpheus and Euridice* and I was slightly critical of some of the costumes she did because she would have them zipped up at the back. She wanted to have a high neck and didn't want to have tights and a leotard because she wanted to avoid the line that would make. I argued that the line was better than seeing the zips but she disagreed. I was also unsure about the Elysian Fields scene when all the garments were made of chiffon which I wasn't keen on for the men.

The set was beautiful, a grey saucer, absolutely wonderful.

Top *Costume drawings for the ballet Act 2.*
Above *Costume drawing for the female chorus Act 1.*

ORPHEUS AND EURIDICE

La Forza del Destino

Giuseppe Verdi (libretto by Francesco Maria Piave), *Director:* John Dexter
2 May 1975, The Paris Opera House.

The libretto asks for: a room hung with damask and decorated in the style of the eighteenth century; the kitchen of an inn; the façade of a church and the entrance to a convent; the interior of a monastery; a forest; a drawing room in Italy; a military encampment; the interior of the convent and a cloister garden; a valley crossed by a stream and flanked by steep cliffs; a cave.

JH: This was a revolutionary production for Paris because there was so little set. The scene changes in *La Forza del Destino* would have gone on forever if I'd tried to do them naturalistically, so I decided that everything would take place on a paved floor which looked like stones and that we would fly in abstract sculptural shapes. I took Goya's paintings in the 'Disasters of War' series as the basis for the design because, like *La Forza del Destino*, there's such a feeling of battles and war in his work and the mixture of people – the aristocracy, the army, gypsies – are there in the paintings too. I had some very powerful lights and the way we lit the stage was also very influenced by Goya's paintings.

The Paris Opera is vast and even more beautiful than Covent Garden, and it has a huge stage. I set a big rostrum on a rake with an entrance at the back and with blacks all around it. There was another entrance downstage, paved like a walkway. All the changes were choreographed and John Dexter made them work rhythmically throughout the opera. For the battle scene we simply had four huge cannon brought in at the back, and the church interior was made using just an arch, a huge hanging crucifix and a procession of monks. Initially the Paris Opera said we couldn't have the big rostrum because it would take too long to strike, but on the first night I struggled out through the crowd at the end and went round to the stage door, which can't have taken more than ten minutes, and the stage was already completely bare as if the opera had never taken place. John later used the same principle to do *The Carmelites* at the Met, which made a big breakthrough there because the audiences had never seen an opera done with practically no scenery before.

The Paris Opera had had the costume drawings for months but nothing had been done when I got there. They'd been busy on something else and didn't seem to have budgeted for us, so I was asked to look through the wardrobes and see if I could find anything from past productions. It was like Bluebeard's Castle, I would open a door and out would come all these amazing costumes from other operas. I came across some uniforms that were absolutely the right colour for soldiers of the period and, although it turned out they had been made for women, it was quicker to alter them for men than make new ones. I managed to get a lot of costumes for the gypsies from an old production of *Carmen* and the principals' costumes were made by the wardrobe.

John Dexter: Jocelyn's work on *La Forza del Destino* was wonderful. That was the best nineteenth century opera I did and the production worked as it was intended to.

FORZA DEL DESTINA - PARIS OPERA - 1975

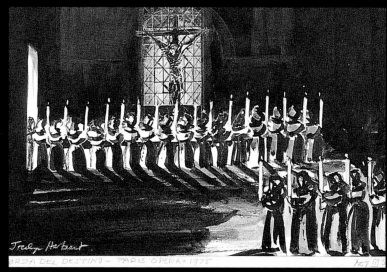

Facing page *Drawing for the interior of the monastery.* Above *Action pictures for* La Forza del Destino.

Lulu

Alban Berg, *Director:* John Dexter
18 March 1977, The Metropolitan Opera, New York.

The opera needs: a painter's studio; a drawing room in Lulu's house; the dressing room of a theatre; a room in Dr. Schön's home; a gambling salon in Paris; a garret in London.

Facing page anticlockwise *Four costume drawings for Lulu; costume drawing for The Countess Geschwitz.*

Below drawings left to right *Lulu Act 1; Geschwitz Act 4; Lulu Act 5; poster Act 3.*

JH: *Lulu* is a very intimate opera, there are only ever about six people on stage, and it was a big terror doing it in such a huge place. At the Met the singers are usually a minimum of fifty feet away from the audience because there's twenty feet between the prompt box[1] and the setting line and the orchestra pit is at least thirty feet across. In order to reduce the distance from fifty to thirty feet, I invented two trucks which came forward alternately over the prompt box. While one was out on stage the other was behind the scenes having its set changed.

I used drapes a lot in this production. For Schön's house I used them to make it seem opulent, and I added a spiral staircase which provided an extra entrance from above and worked well because it meant he could be up there listening and looking at what was going on below. Berg had intended there to be a film of Lulu's imprisonment but I did drawings and projections instead. When we first did *Lulu*, Berg's widow still wasn't allowing the whole of the third act to be performed but the completed opera was done when the Met revived the production. I think both *Lulu* and *Mahagonny* were quite tough on the Met audiences; I don't know which they disliked most, but they were, nevertheless, great successes.

1 *The prompt box is in the centre of the stage, clearly visible to the audience, and is there for the benefit of the singers.*

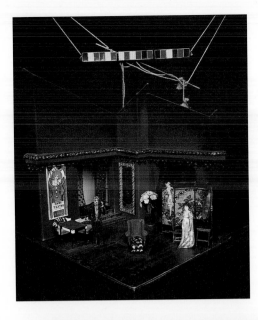

Facing page *Photograph of the model showing Lulu's house
Scene 2.*

Left *Photographs and sketch of the* Lulu *model.*

Bottom left *Production photograph of the Attic showing The
Countess Geschwitz (Tatiana Troyanos) in front of Lulu's
portrait, Act 5, Scene 2.*

Below *Production photograph of The Countess Geschwitz
(Tatiana Troyanos) Act 4.*
Photos: J. Heffernan

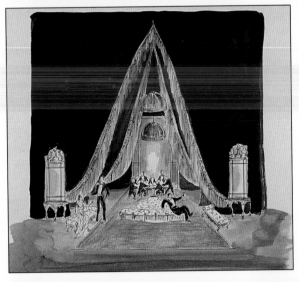

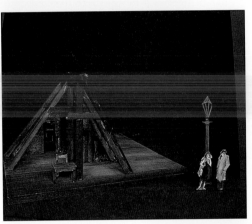

Die Entführung aus dem Serail

Wolfgang Amadeus Mozart (libretto by Bretzner), *Director:* John Dexter
12 October 1979, The Metropolitan Opera, New York.

The opera needs: the exterior of Pasha Selim's palace; the palace garden; a courtyard of the palace; a square outside the palace.

JH: The Met is vast, and the real problem there is how to use the stage and bring it nearer to the audience, particularly for an intimate opera like this. This was the first production that I'd ever done in a painterly way and I chose to set the opera on an island, surrounded by sea and sky.

The first time I ever went to see the Met I'd been shown the cyc which unrolls very gradually like magic and goes all the way round the stage, and I decided to use it for *The Entführung*. It had never been used to its full extent before and no-one knew if it could be lit properly but in the end we discovered it was possible and it looked perfect.

I had looked at a lot of Persian miniatures and noticed how often they use an extraordinary sudden brilliance of colour in a mass of blue, and I decided to pick this up in the set. I was impressed by the different blues of the tiles and also by the incredible doorways in the paintings and so I built up a set which used very simple minaret shapes in blue and white. I made a model and sprayed it using stencils cut with a mesh of tiny holes, turning the stencils all the time so that the blue and white blended and built up shadows, and I used the same process for a huge frontdrop which we used at the beginning and between the acts. The Met has marvellous workshops and all the people working in them are painters so they were delighted with the set and reproduced it wonderfully. It was the kind of design where, if you fudged it, you had to start all over again. I had a cut-out for the temple at the back, with a wall in front of it. Later the wall was flown out, leaving the little house and garden with a brilliant red fence in the midst of the blue and white so that the red was as startling as the colour in the Persian tiles.

I regret that I stuck too closely to the Persian paintings when I did the costumes because in them the people wear every kind of different colour. I didn't like the way the opera looked in the last scene because I'd used too many colours – all based on pinks and reds – and realised afterwards that it would have been better to have kept to blues to prevent them being too dominant.

David Reppa[1]: Jocelyn's instincts are theatrical rather than operatic. A lot of opera designers go for the spectacular and I've never known her do that. The simplicity of her set for *The Entführung* was rare for the Met audience and it came as a surprise to them; it always got a hand when the curtain came up. It was almost magical and made the opera come alive because of its freshness. She made a big, big stage look small so that attention was always focused exactly where it should have been.

We had never used the house roller cyc like that before and it took some time to get rid of the shadows of the scenery on it. The singers, other than those entering downstage, came up through a trap in the floor upstage between the cut-out and the cyc. We had to duplicate the Arabian fretwork of Jocelyn's model so we made four or five six-foot square stencils and sprayed them until we achieved all the little dots and squares. There were places where the dots were pretty much double exposed and the variations really gave the set a vibrancy and a wonderful quality – almost of movement – which was an extraordinary effect to create from absolutely flat scenery.

In a production like that where everything is so clean it's very hard to hide the joins in the scenery, and the hinges had to be countersunk. The opening scene with the garden wall and the fig tree was a problem because the hardware kept showing. Unfortunately scenery in an opera house does have to be folded and put away, and there was a maintenance problem on *The Entführung* because there were always fingerprints where the stage hands picked the scenery up to move it – any stage is a dirty place to work.

I will never be able to think of the garden scene without Jocelyn's red fence; that touch was what

really put it all together. The consistency with which the evening was handled from beginning to end was wonderful; she didn't give the audience literally Persian tiles, she evoked the feeling of them perfectly. It was a way of doing Mozart in a totally contemporary style.

Facing page *Court official.*

Above *First sketches.*

1 *Resident Designer at the Metropolitan Opera.*

Above *Members of the Hareem.*
Facing page *Production photographs.*
Photos: *J. Heffernan*

Rise and Fall of the City of Mahagonny

Kurt Weill (text and lyrics by Bertolt Brecht, translated by David Drew and Michael Geliot),
Director: John Dexter
16 November 1979, The Metropolitan Opera, New York.

*The text asks for: a large lorry in very bad condition which comes to a stop in a desolate place; a
projection showing view of a metropolis and a photomontage of men's faces; a quay near
Mahagonny, a signpost and a price-list; a street map of Mahagonny; a projection giving statistics
about crime and currency fluctuations in Mahagonny, and seven different price-lists; the Do As You
Like Tavern; a white cloud which travels back and forth across the sky, printed notices; a projection
of a map of the hurricane path; a country road; under a sign, 'Loving', a bare room set on a platform;
a sign, 'Fighting', a boxing ring; a sign, 'Drinking'; a courtroom in a tent, suggesting an operating
theatre; a projection of Mahagonny and an electric chair; a projection of Mahagonny in flames.*

JH: This design was very influenced by various Brechtian productions I'd seen and I used the
traditional half-curtain. The problem is that in trying to answer the demands of the text, as in *Mother
Courage*, the designer inevitably comes up with some of the same solutions as Brecht's company
found. It's necessary to find the right style – ironic and poetic at the same time.

John Dexter: I had to do Brecht at the Met, it was the whole point of being there, its raison d'être. I
couldn't have done it with anyone but Jocelyn, and I wouldn't have wanted to; I felt we solved all the
problems of doing *Mahagonny* in that space. There was tension when the chorus master insisted on a
full chorus for the brothel scene even though Jocelyn and I thought it was wrong but then Lotte Lenya
came to a rehearsal – she's a tough lady – and she got it changed.

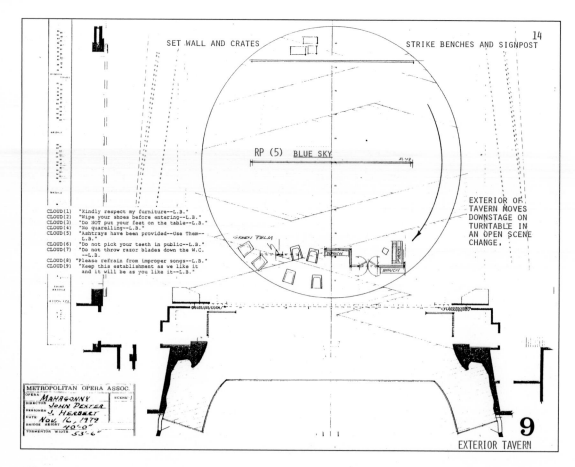

Left *Plan of Met stage showing scene changes.*
Facing page *Storyboard for* Mahagonny.

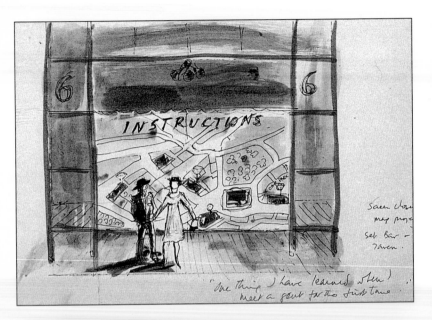

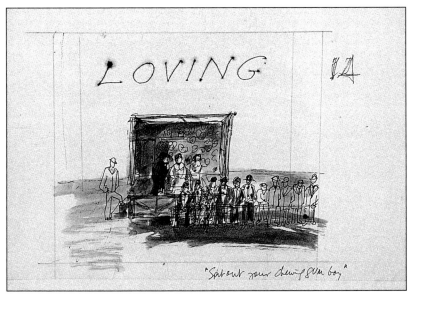

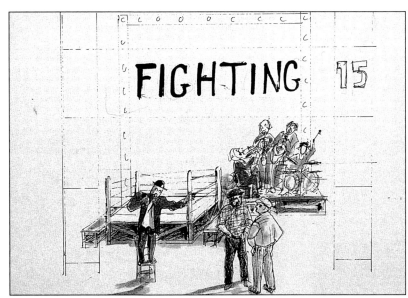

Storyboard for Mahagonny.

Facing page *Production photographs of Mahagonny.*
Photos: J. Heffernan

Above *The model showing the half-curtain and permanent frame structure with scene numbers and microphones.*

Left *Model of the Do As You Like Tavern showing projection screen and permanent frame structure.* *Photos: anon*

194

Top row from facing page to this page *Begbick, Moses, female costume; Production photograph of Teresa Stratas (Jenny); Chorus sketch.*

Bottom row *Female costume, Fatty, Jenny; Production photographs showing the Court and Drinking scenes.*
Photos: J. Heffernan

From left to right *Masks for the three forms in which Orpheus appeared: the Actor, the Mime and the Puppet.* Photos: Sandra Lousada

Costume drawing for Orpheus.

The Mask of Orpheus

Harrison Birtwistle (libretto by Peter Zinovieff), *Director:* David Freeman
21 May 1986, The Coliseum (world première).

The Mask of Orpheus *has a very complex structure and some of the demands of the libretto were* *unachievable. Amongst the elements asked for were suns, rivers, a golden carriage flying through* *the air, the Underworld ('the arches') and 'the essence of mountains'.*

JH: *The Mask of Orpheus* was one of the most exciting things I've ever been involved in. Normally when I'm designing opera I play the music all the time, but in this case there was no music to hear because it was all still being written down in notation. I'd been working on it for some time before we heard tapes of the Passing Clouds music, and we did eventually have an orchestral run-through but that was quite late on when we were already rehearsing and about to move into the theatre.

I read and read the libretto and for a long time I couldn't make head or tail of it. Harry Birtwistle had told me there would be an aura of electronic music into which the orchestral music suddenly entered through speakers so that the sound was linked. Through talking to him about his music and the ritualistic aspect of *The Mask of Orpheus*, the repeats and ceremonies, I began to realise that it was absolutely pointless to attempt any kind of illustration because that would only have been confusing. The opera is not just one story, but the telling and re-telling of many different myths. Zinovieff had written the structure, the three acts with the ceremonies being repeated, making a play on the number three throughout; each principal character appeared in three forms, the Actor, the Mime and the Puppet. Gradually I got a vision of very clear entrances and repeated ceremonies, although the music made it difficult to make some of the ceremonial entrances.

It was important to have a strong visual change for the second act when the action altered from Earth to Hell. At the Coliseum there is no lift or trap as the canteen is underneath the stage. My first design was based on a circle surrounded by a ramp with a central disc which could either be raised and slanted or lowered flat and so could create a spiral entrance to the Underworld. Given money and good hydraulics it might have worked, but I never finalised it because it was too expensive and David Freeman didn't like it. After that we went through endless ideas and I made countless models and was getting more and more miserable because I felt it was moving further and further away from what I wanted to do. Suddenly the budget was cut from £100,000 to £25,000 and we were asked if we thought we could still do the opera. It was quite a relief to me to have a smaller budget because it meant we had to forget the ideas we'd been working on and I went back to my original circle but did it in a much simpler way without any of the hydraulics.

We put down a wooden floor which stayed throughout the opera and which had a circle cut into it. I had strong feelings from the libretto about the need for a river in the first act. I did it very simply, using a long piece of painted raw silk which came down from the flies as a brilliant green shape of grass was unrolled beneath it. The blue of the river and the very bright yellowy green of the carpet were visually important, like the red sun and the blue sky, and needed to be clear cut.

For the second act, when Orpheus goes into the Underworld, the sections of the circle in the centre of the floor were removed to reveal metal grids underneath, which were lit from below and formed the path he took in Hell. The River Styx was made in the same way and Charon's boat was based on a Japanese picture; the boat was a lovely shape and it was possible for Charon to walk in it and move it, although in the end there wasn't enough rehearsal time to get it right. The ladders in the Underworld were there entirely to create a feeling of depth, of being low down below the earth. In the model, when I had the idea for the ladders, I hung little figures on them and found that it worked terribly well. The Puppets in Hell (they're called Puppets in the script, but the word doesn't really describe them) became very big to create the sense that Orpheus was getting smaller and smaller as he went deeper into the Underworld; the people he met in Hell were gradated, the first ones he met were bigger than he was, the next bigger still and the last three, the Gods, were enormous. Then, as Orpheus left the Underworld, the Puppets he met got smaller again.

There were dozens of different Puppets mentioned all the time in the libretto and originally there

Orpheus' head floating down the river. Photo: Catherine Ashmore

was talk of using articulated puppets and then huge puppets; we just couldn't see our way through it all so we gradually had to come down to essentials. The three forms in which the principal actors appeared had to look alike but be different. Harry wanted masks from the beginning and there was no way I could do the trios successfully without them and still keep the idea that it was the same person in a different form.

The masks for this were quite different from the ones we made for *The Oresteia* and we were able to make much freer shapes. The Actors had to sing so theirs were conditioned by that and we made their half-masks first. The masks for the Mimes, who didn't have to sing or speak, came next; these were full-masks but based on the half-masks of the singers. To achieve the Puppets we made the head and the full-mask bigger and the whole figure a head taller than usual but kept the proportions of the rest of the body the same size as a normal human being. The wigs were made using string, ribbon and cord.

I tried to develop a timeless costume and wanted a non-modern feel which was definitely un-English. It was difficult to find something very simple that was archaic and not intrusively Greek. I looked at books from Brazil, Africa, China, medieval illustrations – everything – and picked things I could adapt. I didn't reproduce exactly what I found, but I made use of details and evolved something that was unidentifiable and not from a specific period, using shapes with an other-worldly feel to them.

It took me a while to find the right combination of colours for the costumes, but all the little scribbles I did were bright colours and they needed to be electric to stand out in the very empty space. The opera began with the sun and I wanted Orpheus to become part of it, whilst Euridice's colour was the same as the river. The libretto said Orpheus should be in red, Euridice in blue and Aristaeus in green, but I didn't want Orpheus to be in red so I found a lovely orangey colour. The priests wore dimmer colours except for bright orange details – there was always a link. In Hell everything was dark except for the orange figure of Orpheus wandering around inside.

If I did *The Mask of Orpheus* again I wouldn't change very much, but it would be important to get more rehearsal time to solve the technical problems. The moving suns, the snakes and the last act all needed more work, and I would have liked to improve on the costumes, particularly the Puppets. In opera you only get one dress rehearsal and there were so many things that could have gone wrong in this one that, when something didn't work, I just said to cut it and not waste any more time on it. The first performance could quite easily have been a disaster and quite a few things did go wrong. We didn't have the sun going up in the opening scene until practically the last day, which was very nerve - wracking. There was also supposed to be a small sun in the river scene which had to travel gradually across the back. The technical people knew about it and had said it wouldn't be a problem but when they produced it it was the most awful sort of box which wobbled about and looked ridiculous, so I cut it. In Act 3 there's a mountain (which I made using a cut-out and its shadow) with a head floating down the river behind it and unfortunately that was never rehearsed properly, but, on the few times when it happened as it should always have done, it was magical.

Facing page *Early drawings for* The Mask of Orpheus.

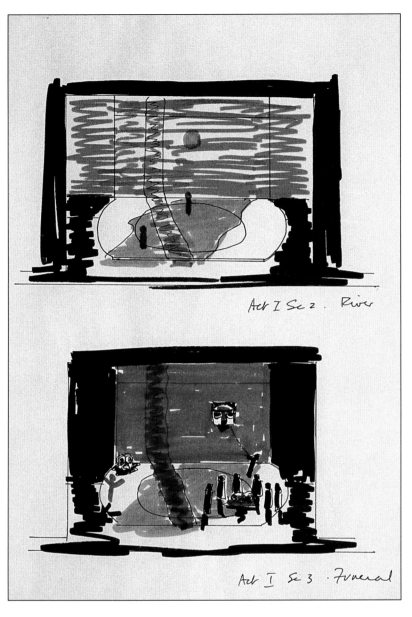

Act I Sc 2 . River

Act I Sc 3 . Funeral

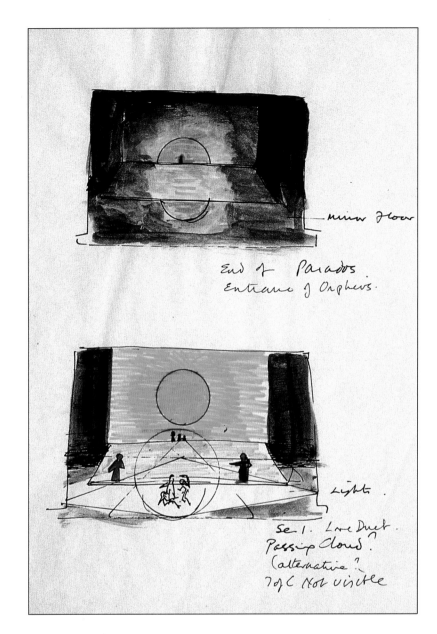

miror floor

End of Parados.
Entrance of Orpheus.

Lights.

Sc 1 . Love Duet.
Passing Cloud ?
(alternative ?)
Top Not visible

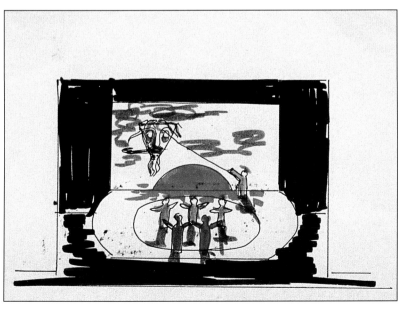

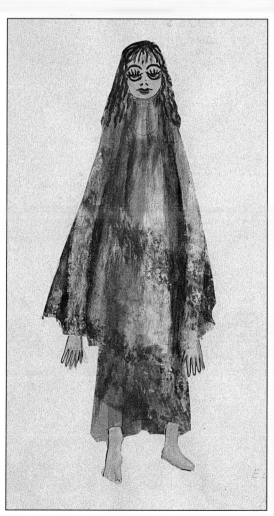

Facing page *Animal masks (eagle and dog). Costume drawings for Euridice; the Actor, the Mime and the Puppet.*
Above *Masks for Euridice and Aristaeus; the Actor, the Mime and the Puppet.* Photos: Sandra Lousada

Production photographs. Photos: Catherine Ashmore

Production photographs. Photos: Catherine Ashmore

Jocelyn Herbert, 1986.
Photo: Lindsay Anderson

Contributions from colleagues

Edited from interviews

Contributions from Colleagues

Edited from interviews

Margaret Harris, designer and teacher

British theatre design went through a low time until Nigel Playfair, who was a great friend of Jocelyn's father [A.P. Herbert, whose plays at the Lyric, Hammersmith, were Jocelyn's introduction to the theatre], began to develop it again. Lovat Fraser was the first designer to get rid of all the brocade and rabbit fur and do things with a sharp clear outline. He and Diaghilev's ballet at the Coliseum were tremendous influences on we Motleys [Margaret 'Percy' Harris, Sophie Harris, Elizabeth Montgomery] and we all three taught at the London Theatre Studio. We, through Michel Saint-Denis, had a big influence on Jocelyn and her generation and then she taught at my Theatre Design Course and had a great influence on Hayden Griffin and his contemporaries. I don't think Jocelyn likes teaching, but she's very good at it and extremely direct. She will say what she thinks, but is always constructive and never cruel. She was very tough with Hayden because she could see he had talent and, eventually, he did something she liked and from then on they got on very well. Now Hayden teaches at the school, so there's a continuous line of development.

Jocelyn was a very good student at the LTS, the same lively, warm person that she is now. I remember her costumes for *Juanita*, which were very successful, based on Goya's 'Disasters of War'; she caught the style, colour and the feeling of them without being slavishly imitative. The design students had a lot of classes on the technical and practical side and they were set projects which I and the other instructors would work out with them and then Michel would come and criticize and talk. He required a costume to follow the sketch accurately and at a costume parade he would say to a design student, "There are four buttons here and only three buttons on the drawing. Why?" If it was because the proportions were better or another good reason he would accept it, but he would always notice a discrepancy.

Michel had a tremendous influence on George Devine because he had worked with him for so long, but later on George branched off by himself. He too was very accurate in everything he did but he was much more anxious to allow every artist working on a production to develop themselves. He used to say to students, "I don't want to tell you what to do. I want you to do it and then I'll criticize it." He would be very much the same when working professionally and one would work very closely with him. He would always have a basic idea about what he wanted and within that he would let you go free. Both Michel and George believed that the most important thing was the play and then the actors, and Jocelyn absorbed that from them and I think she has always stuck to it.

In the early days the director was very much the boss, but now the link between director and designer has become much closer. It began to happen between Glen Byam Shaw and myself because we worked together for so long, but I didn't have as much control over the text and the way he approached the production as Jocelyn does now with the directors she works with. They respect her so much and I think she influences them more than they influence her.

There are two kinds of stage designers: there are designers and there are decorators. The big difficulty that I think Jocelyn has solved so well is to remain simple but to maintain enough decorative feeling to keep her sets alive and, where appropriate, beautiful. She is a real puritan, everything she does is always absolutely pure but always beautiful too. A minimal set can be boring, but with her it never is because she has an amazing talent in choosing exactly the right elements that are exciting without in any way being distracting.

Suria Magito [Saint-Denis], teacher and specialist in masks

My first meeting with Jocelyn was when she was a student at the LTS. She was very exciting to work with, very imaginative and inventive. She was born into an artistic family and had always moved in circles with painters, poets, musicians and writers so there was an interesting formation there already and that gave her a certain amount of freedom. It took some time for her to move away from the idea of the painter as designer, and it was something which she ultimately learnt from Michel Saint-Denis, who was fascinated by architecture. Michel taught her freedom and discipline: how to discipline freedom. She was a very intimate and true friend and, of the design students, the closest to him.

Jocelyn's work has changed over the years and she's become freer and more unconventional. She's had tremendous success and is a most original designer and now does things she wouldn't have dared fifteen or twenty years ago. Gradually, as you grow older and work more by yourself you come into your own. It's difficult to say what would have happened if George Devine were still alive; if you're very much in love with a person you do listen to what they say. She sometimes uses criticism, but she's not absolutely bound to it which is what I mean by freedom. She makes mistakes sometimes, and sometimes not – after all, she's an artist.

Hugh Casson, architect and designer

I first worked with Jocelyn in 1953 when I was designing William Walton's opera, *Troilus and Cressida*, at Covent Garden. Malcolm Sargent was conducting and George Devine was directing. I saw little of Sargent but I enjoyed the company of George virtually every day throughout rehearsals. He was splendid to work with, clear, positive, even-tempered and uncompromising. He used to tell you, for instance, he wanted a singer to stand "Four feet above stage level and seven feet back... and that doesn't mean eight!" You knew where you were, and as a new boy to theatre design I needed all the expertise he could provide. Jocelyn was his amanuensis. She had a notebook, sensible shoes to run errands in, a faultless sensitivity to his need to keep quiet at times but always to be there when wanted. She was also beautiful and funny. Beneath her charm she possessed a healthy quantity of flint and would never give way on matters she believed to be important. The unimportant, she had little respect for.

She didn't waste time messing about in café society or talking on the radio or any of the things artists tend to get diverted by. I would guess she's always disapproved of the cream puff side of theatre and as a result her work has made strong dents where they were needed. She is also a deeply modest girl... the modesty of a true professional. A true professional, I believe, is always a radical, and Jocelyn has always been a radical designer. She believes in theatre as a social and political weapon and is able to be uncompromising without being dogmatic – wisely since, in the end, it's dogma which destroys nations and people. She doesn't waver and she manages to be serious without ever being solemn. She's naturally very loyal and her heart's as big as a house with room inside for everyone... except pseuds, of course. Most endearing of all her qualities is perhaps the warmth of her personality. To sit next to her throughout those weeks of rehearsal was like sitting next to a radiator.

Peggy Ashcroft, actress, former member of the Council of the English Stage Company

I think Jocelyn has been the heart of The Royal Court. She and George Devine worked almost as one person, and it was a sort of miracle that their theatre, with its 'right to fail', succeeded. Without The Court, plays such as Wesker's and Osborne's just would not have been done. All those people – John Osborne, Tony Richardson, Lindsay Anderson, Bill Gaskill – were close to Jocelyn and, inevitably, she had an influence on them. There has been the influence of her work with the directors, but also her great personal influence throughout The Court structure. Most people who came into that sphere had careers to carve and they remained part of The Court for as long as it worked and then went their separate ways, but Jocelyn was otherwise and The Court, to her, was a cause. She was as much part of The Court as The Court was part of her, like a family. Everyone there turned to Jocelyn. The very recounting of her output since George died shows her strength and fortitude and her determination to continue their work, and that is what has sustained her. After George's death she joined the Council, which she took deeply seriously. I was also on the Council and the one thing you knew was that she would have a quite definite opinion; she wasn't inflexible, but everyone recognised she had a steadfast point of view on any particular subject.

Working with her on *The Seagull* was a wonderfully happy experience. There was never anything put on stage by Jocelyn that didn't contribute absolutely to the main thrust of the production. She is able to understand character so well that she could only contribute to an actor's performance by her design because there would be nothing that wasn't agreed and understood between her, the actor and the director.

She's the most modest and unassuming person that it's possible to meet. Beckett's friendship gives you her measure. She expends an enormous amount of energy on her friends and fellow workers, and the quality that she has above all is her *joie de vivre*. Her whole life is generous and giving, whether it's looking after her family, giving hospitality to companies after first nights or advising young people and her assistant designers. She's a very, very rare person.

Oscar Lewenstein, former member of the Council of the English Stage Company

The people at The Royal Court, including Jocelyn and George Devine, were very untheoretical people and they seldom voiced a thought-out ideological attitude – they may have had one but they didn't speak in those terms. Jocelyn isn't a particularly logical woman, so her influence didn't come through an intellectual laying out of ideas, but in more subtle ways. Her instincts are very, very good, she can recognise the bogus on stage and her feelings are invariably right. She personifies and combines the best qualities of The Court: a certain integrity, a certain social concern – but of a muddled kind – a dedication to serving the writers and to working collectively.

Tony Richardson, director

A lot of the pre-Jocelyn period at The Royal Court was very much based on theory, which I disliked. When we started, George Devine wanted to bring in ideas which had been current at the London Theatre Studio where he and the Motleys had taught, and we began with a permanent surround for the stage and there was even talk of a basic costume which could be adapted for each play. However much the Motleys were open to new ways of working – and they were to a large extent – they were also very much bound by practice because by then they'd done so many things. They had done progressive theatre in the thirties, working with John Gielgud and Michel Saint-Denis, when the emphasis was more on finding new ways to stage classics than on new writing.

We were doing plays by writers working in very different styles and Jocelyn was a much more contemporary designer. I think she had a stronger visual sense than either George or Michel, and she had lived more in the art world as distinct from the world of theatre. The Motleys were a marvellous influence, but Jocelyn was certainly a new spirit and she had a better sense of colour. She was very beautiful and passionate and full of life and was working killing hours as a scene painter in the workshops; it was obvious she was longing to design something and it was my idea to do *The Chairs* with her. After that she was in constant demand.

By the time she arrived at The Court she'd been away from the theatre for a long while, and possibly this made it easier for her to respond to the new writing. She began to practise design rather late and, instead of starting young and experimenting in different styles, she had already done a lot of thinking and feeling about what the theatre should be. Another point is that she was never under a commercial pressure, she didn't *have* to be a designer. The world she comes out of is one of total theatre, where the director, the designer and the writer are working together for a unified concept, and her work isn't born out of conflict but from collaboration.

You wouldn't go to Jocelyn if you wanted a perfectly realised, realistic Verdi opera – the sort of thing Lila de Nobile did absolutely sublimely because it was based on impeccable research and detail. Jocelyn proceeds in a different way and, although she does do research, it is always subordinated to her vision of the text and the director's conception of it. She is a much purer designer than most, absolutely focused and precise; what you get from her is a pared-down design, the simplest vision that is right for the play. To say her work is minimal is wrong because she does things which are rich and stunning if that is what is needed. *Luther* was easy because we both liked simplicity and bare stages. It was in the same tradition as *The Changeling*, where there was nothing that wasn't absolutely necessary. There were precise visual images against a vast background that was vaguely suggestive of a medieval world. We have always tried not to follow all the stage directions slavishly but to see the vision the author wanted and try and translate them into precise physical terms. She is the designer with whom I've most enjoyed collaborating and has a better sense of the heart of a play and the author's vision than anyone I've ever worked with.

Bill Gaskill, director

I vividly remember my first impressions of Jocelyn. I was invited to a Boat Race party at George Devine's house on the river by Hammersmith Bridge and I remember saying, "Who is that wonderful girl?" She must have been about forty then, incredibly young-looking, and wearing a white Arran sweater which John Dexter later told me was the one Joan Plowright wore in *Roots*.

The climate around The Court was very emotional and people's personal relationships were woven into the fabric of the work there, but there was also a certain stability of theatrical values. It was an inheritance from the days of Michel Saint-Denis. Glen Byam Shaw, George Devine, the Redgraves and John Gielgud were all drawn together partly because they shared Michel's dream of a more serious theatre, and many of them had worked with him on *Three Sisters*. They were the people who dominated the British theatre. It was very glamorous for us, the younger generation, because all the famous names we'd always known were suddenly living people with whom we had contact. The opportunities were enormous and George opened that world up to us.

I hadn't seen any of Jocelyn's work when I met her, but soon after I remember seeing *The Chairs*, which was magical and atmospheric. It was a new kind of play and the production had a marvellous quality of unity. After that we all wanted to work with Jocelyn and in those days I would have worked on anything with her. She was designing for the first time, but with the experience of life and maturity which we, obviously, didn't have, and which was very rich. We could trust her; the whole aesthetic basis of The Court came from her and no-one else. *Roots* was not a typical play for Jocelyn to do; one associated her with a rather poetic drama, whereas the Wesker play is realistic, and I think it showed real imagination on John Dexter's part to ask her to do it.

Mother Courage was a mistake because I tried to imitate Brecht's production and Jocelyn more or less copied Teo Otto's sets exactly. She didn't bring anything new to the play (except for a rather beautiful curtain with a map of leather stretched on it and tied on four poles) and I don't think I did either, but it's a great and wonderful work and it had to be done in English. I think one of Jocelyn's few weaknesses is that she sometimes gets overawed by the great. It's something I've suffered from in my life, too. When you see something you admire unreservedly, you invest it with total authority. Jocelyn's version of Brechtian has always been softer, more poetic than The Berliner Ensemble's. *Baal* was an early play and in some ways it's a romantic work so her response was right for it. What she used was a sense of evocation of nature, which I don't think Brecht was interested in at all. Jocelyn gets that from the English romantic tradition and her designs for plays like *Baal* and the Wesker *Trilogy* were some of the most beautiful things she ever did.

There aren't many designers with whom one can prepare work over so long a period or so closely as one can with Jocelyn. She has a certain aristocratic authority about her and is a steadying influence on a director – she doesn't flirt with ideas that are nothing to do with the play. She is marvellously flexible, and because of that she usually gets her own way in the end; she very rarely has head-on conflicts and will always give and then find her own way round a problem. She's very patient and gentle with actors and people respond to her and trust her. She is the only designer I know who is delighted when a director scraps a piece of scenery. That is because she understands the whole basis of theatre; most designers are in some sense decorative and want to show they exist by putting something on stage whereas Jocelyn is a non-decorative person. Most of the time designers say, "I want this because this is how I imagined it and how it has got to be," but Jocelyn would never say that, and that is terribly rare.

John Dexter, director

When I joined The Royal Court Jocelyn was the staff painter and our conversations were largely practical; she talked my language, which was more than most people there did. I saw *The Chairs* and had watched her in the workshop and then I asked her to do *Purgatory*.

I came from weekly rep, where you have a limited number of flats which are painted and over-painted until the paint flakes off, so the design ideas at The Court were new to me. I wanted to get away from naturalism and realism. I did two Sunday night productions without decor: *Yes and After*, with a stripped down stage, and *The Kitchen*. These pointed me in the direction of provoking the audience to think for themselves and use their imagination.

The model which Jocelyn did for *Roots* was perfect. The only thing I said was that I always wanted to be aware of the space outside, the emptiness of it. Jocelyn went up to Dusty Wesker's and I worked from the text: Jocelyn needed to go and I needed *not* to go. Real time and natural time are both at the service of theatrical time when you're doing a play, so the pacing of *Roots* was very simple. Jenny Beales had to fry liver and onions – it was a practical problem of how long it needed to cook and serve and eat it. Practical problems were about all you had time to solve, and in solving those in that sort of play, you tend to discover the play itself. When we came to do *Chicken Soup With Barley*, I wanted to set the play in an East End basement rather than in the attic as Arnold Wesker had written it. It helped to convey a sort of submerged society and intensified the family feeling – the constant coming and going of people visiting one another, which doesn't happen anymore. We did two weeks talking, looking at the groundplan, playing with bits of cardboard. We had to 'sort out the plumbing,' the geography of the place. You do that with any play, no matter how abstract. *I'm Talking About Jerusalem* was more difficult than *Roots* and *Chicken Soup* and it needed much more light and space. In a way it was the most beautiful piece of design in the *Trilogy* because it opened out the space much more than the other two.

The difference between working with Jocelyn and another designer is the 'rightness' of everything. One never has the feeling that she is trying to impose her design personality on a play – that, of course, comes through anyway – nor is she trying to make a design statement. The design is always at the service of the play. If Jocelyn likes what I'm doing it's reassuring – if she doesn't, I question what I've done.

Arnold Wesker, playwright

Jocelyn designed the initial productions of my first five plays. The *Trilogy* is conventionally structured, but it takes a family over twenty years, from 1936 to 1956, and that was fairly novel in those days. The structures of *The Kitchen* and *Chips with Everything* were innovative. I knew you could put a kitchen and thirty two characters on a stage. I really felt that anything was possible. I trusted both Jocelyn and John Dexter because they felt they were there to serve the play; a work of theatre is an individual vision of experience and they respected that. I believe it is the responsibility of the playwright to conceive his play as totally as possible, and I try to make my work director-proof and, to some extent, designer-proof. Much of my work is autobiographical and I have very vivid images in my mind of what I want. Jocelyn's sets were aesthetically stunning and absolutely in keeping with the spirit of the plays and their reality.

Jocelyn's approach taught me about design from the word go and she gave me a taste for austerity. She coped brilliantly with the problems of *Roots*. She started out with everything on the page and threw all her ideas down, but the final design was the result of whittling away until she was left with the bare minimum. For theatrical reasons, Dexter's suggestion that we set *Chicken Soup* in a basement seemed a good one and the half-windows allowed us to have one or two stage managers running backwards and forwards to create the impression of a big demonstration gathering. It didn't correspond to autobiographical reality, but nevertheless we could just as easily have been living in a basement in Fashion Street as in the attic.

There was tension when John, Jocelyn and I were working on *The Merchant* in 1977 and I was, finally, disappointed by her designs for that. I'd very deliberately called for two elements, the dark and gloom of the ghetto and the colour and vivacity of Venice. I wanted those two contrasts, but I don't think I got them in the end although there were moments when Andy Phillips' lighting was full of rich atmosphere and the sets looked like Rembrandt paintings. I don't think the design for that production was as successful as the one Christopher Moreley did when the play was done in Birmingham. Apart from *The Merchant*, my memory of Jocelyn is of someone who was always very supportive.

Lindsay Anderson, director

In 1959, when I was going to direct *Serjeant Musgrave's Dance*, George Devine suggested I might talk to Jocelyn Herbert. She existed in a mysterious way in the workshop, which I don't think I ever visited, painting scenery. She wasn't established as a designer by any means and I knew very little about the theatre then. I found her immediately sympathetic and intelligent and authoritative in her own sphere, and I had no hesitation whatsoever in asking her to design the play. We had, and always have had, our moments of healthy abrasion; they're just part of a very good working relationship.

From the beginning it was perfectly apparent that Jocelyn had the qualities of a remarkable designer. An empty stage would always appeal to her, morally almost more than aesthetically: she doesn't really think there ought to be sets. The better a designer is the less likely it is that their work will be noticed. The English have so little visual sense that, unless a design is spectacular or crude, they don't actually notice whether it's good or bad but have a purely literary response to a play; it's a missing nerve. I think this applies particularly to Jocelyn since her designs are always totally integrated with the play and are an extension of the poetic heart of the text, executed with extreme sensitivity and intuition. She doesn't make claims for herself and it's almost natural that uncultivated critics wouldn't notice her designs.

She is someone who really studies the text and comes up with a design which can accommodate the dramatic demands of the play. That sounds completely elementary, but it's surprising how many designers don't actually do that but instead come up with a spectacular stage picture which is of no practical use. When I went to Poland to direct *Inadmissible Evidence* in 1965 I was given someone who came up with a spectacular design but who had never worked out how the actors could move or where the judge could sit. I had to get Jocelyn to come out and she arrived with all her instruments, her model from the original production and the groundplan. She amazed the Polish staff by getting down on the floor and drawing the whole set out and talking to them. They weren't used to that, they were used to people coming in and handing them a drawing and leaving all the work to them. Jocelyn's down-to-earth professionalism staggered them.

Jocelyn, David Storey and I were a good team because we respected each other and had a certain moral and poetic sense in common. When we lost The Court we lost a centre and I think David has lost a place where he feels at home. He has never been happy writing in a void; like a painter, he saw that particular stage and imagined everything happening in that space. We three worked very closely together and there was an integrated quality of life at The Court which enabled that to happen.

The Court was aiming to rediscover good theatrical style and wanted to establish the kind of simplicity in which each element served the text to the greatest extent. Style is finding a method in direction, design, acting, movement and speech which expresses the essential context and attitude of the play. It has its own kind of refinement, its own characteristics beyond the purely naturalistic, which correspond to the values of the play.

Perhaps there is a tendency to stress the artistic side of Jocelyn's design at the expense of her practicality. David Storey's *The March on Russia*, for instance, called for special treatment when it was decided to perform it at the Lyttelton, on a stage really larger than the author had imagined. Jocelyn built the first floor of the house over the living room, with a bedroom visible throughout the evening. On either side of the house there was a strip of garden. The result was a decor which served the play and also illuminated its poetic subtext. And when we went on tour, we were able to perform on the original set which adapted to fit a number of different stages.

David Storey, playwright

Jocelyn was a revelation to me both in personal and artistic terms, and I've always found her a very inspiring person. She comes from a world of expansiveness, generosity and accessibility, which are qualities I associate her with specifically. I come from the opposite end of the boxing-ring, from a world which, by comparison, felt mean-spirited and destructive and where to be an artist was always an horrendous struggle. I ended up playing professional football to support myself as an artist and I can't say the combination worked; it was something I had to do on my own and initially my experience of the arts and of self-expression was a punitive one. I felt an immediate rapport with Jocelyn, and her world is one that I enormously warm towards but can never feel a part of; there's no barrier between us as people and yet culturally we appeared to have little in common.

As a designer Jocelyn is really an agent, the means through which passes the intention of the production, which is the combination of the director's ideas and the ethos in which the company is working – the building, the people involved and so on. Like a 'cellist or a violinist, there's the text and there's her interpretation of it; she has a mediumistic power and her lack of egoism is a great virtue. She doesn't assert: she absorbs all the elements involved and then expresses them, which is a completely artistic function. Her great gift, apart from intuition, is her identification with the material.

Jocelyn is the designer I would always choose to work with. Her visual instincts are genuinely theatrical and not those of a painter or graphic artist. She's got a remarkable instinct for moving a stage backwards and seeing it in the third dimension all the time, which many designers are, instinctively, unable to do. I suppose her gift as a designer, quite apart from her personality is, in literary terms, her lyricism. It's a visual lyricism which is the unifying element in all her designs, even in those which are simple and austere.

Seeing *Arnold Middleton* [1967] at The Court triggered off a very creative period for me, sparked off by the magic of that particular stage. My plays were not written as a result of The Court atmosphere but because of that one evening watching that lighted box. I really began to understand the importance of the technical side of production when I did *The Contractor*. The day before the first rehearsal I started cutting it but later I had to feed all the material back into the play because, intuitively, I'd matched the dialogue with the action of putting up and taking down the tent. That made the penny drop in terms of the relationship between what was happening on stage technically and the emotional impact that those actions quite unconsciously expressed.

I wrote *Home* immediately after *The Contractor*. *The Contractor* ended with a bare stage except for a white table from which the tent contractor offers his workmen a drink. In my mind's eye that white table on the imaginary Court stage was so evocative that I realised it was the beginning of a play and not just the end, so I just wrote down that there was a white table and two chairs and that someone came and sat in one. That couldn't last very long so someone else came and sat on the other chair and *Home* carried on from there. It wasn't until the middle of the play that I realised it was a lunatic asylum, which came as a surprise to me.

Home was hilarious. The rehearsals were done in the theatre and not in the rehearsal room so the atmosphere was very evocative. Ralph Richardson and John Gielgud were apprehensive. They'd never done a play like *Home* and at the time felt uncertain about their connections with contemporary theatre. Ralph didn't show it because of the pride and strength of his nature, but John was quite open about it. Their anxiety showed itself in their being both garrulous and energised to the extent that Lindsay couldn't control them. It was like being in a carriage with a couple of runaway horses, the driver saying there was nothing he could do and dropping the reins. It was several days before they'd exhausted their initial nervous energy. At one point John said, "I come from a theatrical tradition where it is the actor's privilege to entertain the audience, and that is what I feel I ought to be doing. In this theatre the actor is there to instruct the audience – this is didactic theatre – and I can't do that, it's not my instinct." Eventually, of course, *Home* worked because they were from that tradition and could seduce the audience in that particular way.

From my observation, Jocelyn's presence alone has a reassuring effect on a production. You can see when somebody's standing in a rehearsal whether they're creatively involved with what's going on or merely watching – there's something about the body which conveys it and I think actors are even more conscious of it than authors. Actors sense that she's someone who is inside their own experience and, also, when she talks to them about their costumes there's an immediate rapport. It isn't just a designer discussing what an actor is going to look like, but someone who understands what the actor is conveying and his horrible insecurity at being on stage. That's all a built-in part of Jocelyn so it's an enormous collaborative infusion quite apart from a technical one. She's the embodiment of a tradition which has virtually disappeared now. She just represents something indispensable.

Alan Bates, actor

Many designers put themselves in a position apart from the director, writer and actor. They really should be doing paintings which sell in galleries because they don't always have a lot to do with what's going on in the play. Working with Jocelyn is different. When *Stages* was first mooted, David Storey, Lindsay Anderson and myself went to her house to look at the model and it is quite rare for an actor to have that initial involvement. Jocelyn attended more rehearsals than I've known a designer to do and her unique quality is to be absolutely part of the process of putting the play on. There have been occasions when I've had to time my lines to cross a set because the designer has not been part of the production and has just presented an ego trip of his own, but Jocelyn would never do that. She carries a purity and an identification with what's been written further than any designer I've known and yet she's made a stronger mark than those who are just showing off.

I didn't particularly visualise *Stages* when I read it. The great thing about Jocelyn and Lindsay is that they allow things to evolve and creep up on them. They approach a play almost from underneath and test it and test it and then they suddenly burst through. Jocelyn understood that *Stages* is about a man in a depressed state of mind who is imagining the past. She implied the world of the play with the simplest means and is a conjuror in the sense that theatre people should be. Although the actors who came onto the stage to play with Fenchurch were really there, the fact that the audience could see them approach through the semi-transparent walls showed they were also part of his memory.

The furniture in the play was introduced very gradually. Jocelyn would say, "This is just a rehearsal chair," and Lindsay would look at it and say, "I don't think that's very good, really. Still, we'll use it for now." You'd go on and use it and ten days later Lindsay would say, "I quite like that chair. Does it belong to the theatre?" The chair became the one we kept and I expect she intended that from a long way back. It became the only one I could have used. If you're on stage for a long time with a lot of lines to say, you need to be in a chair you can grasp and clutch and feel at home in so that you've got a little sanctuary. She realises how actors feel, unlike some other designers who have no interest in the actor and might produce a chair at the dress rehearsal. She has an equally sympathetic approach to costumes. The cardigan she provided for me in rehearsals and the chair made me feel that I had a tiny world on stage even though I was exposed all night.

Jocelyn's relationship with Lindsay is like a marriage. Sometimes you hear them both saying, "This is the last time." They quarrel, they shout at each other in front of others and people are appalled, and then you suddenly see them having lunch together and laughing and giggling. There is a collusion of spirit there. Jocelyn's a very gentle person and Lindsay is abrasive but he has the most enormous respect for her. She's unique and stands alone. She is the lesson for young designers.

Samuel Beckett, playwright and director

I had trouble finding a theatre in France for the first production of *Fin de Partie*, so I came to The Royal Court to do it. The atmosphere in the fifties and sixties was very good and everyone was extremely keen. George Devine was omnipresent, the whole heart of the theatre. He and Jocelyn were so deeply involved with the theatre that they carried their involvement into their home. When George directed and acted in the first English version of *Endgame*, I remember going to discuss the set with Jocelyn in The Royal Court's workshops in Chelsea and finding her very striking, but I only got to know her well after George's death. She was deeply shattered when he died but was tremendously brave and very stoical about not showing her grief. I remember going with her to a big Bonnard exhibition at that time, and that we admired the same things. She became my closest friend in England, and she designed all the productions I did at The Royal Court.

Theatre began for me as relaxation. I was writing the *Trilogy* and got blocked and, at the end of *Malone Dies*, I had to have a break from it. I turned to the theatre as one turns to light, needing to write something with a limited shape and space instead of the blackness of a novel. *Waiting for Godot* was written between *Malone Dies* and *The Unnamable*, and was finished in 1948 and, to me, it is an allegro which breaks, pauses, and then the allegro starts again. It was turned down by everyone until 1953 when Roger Blin did a very good production in which I was involved. Giacometti designed the tree for a later production and that worked very well. I think Peter Hall now realises that the set for the first English production was overburdened – I had asked for an empty space with a tree and a stone and he had it cluttered with a complicated labyrinth.

I wrote *Krapp's Last Tape* for Patrick Magee. I hadn't met him, but I'd heard his voice reading texts for the BBC's third programme and was so impressed that I wanted to write a monologue for him. That's how *Krapp* began. Magee was tremendous, a very good actor and I liked working with him. I was fairly involved in George Devine's production, hanging around most of the time, adjusting parts and saying what I thought.

Directing for me is months and months of preparation and it is that, rather than the actual stagework, which is terrible; you have to know every detail in your head and have the text by heart. I was always very happy when I was working with Jocelyn and I don't remember any reserve on her part; she was wholeheartedly in harmony and I thought I was lucky to have her. I remember the trouble she took over the costume for *Footfalls*. It seemed all right to me, but she still found details that were wrong. She took endless pains to get it right. She has great feeling for the work and is very sensitive and doesn't want to bang the nail on the head. Generally speaking, there is a tendency on the part of designers to overstate and this has never been the case with Jocelyn.

Brenda Bruce, actress

I didn't know Jocelyn at all before *Happy Days* although I knew her work. I'd always wanted to do something at The Royal Court, I thought it was my kind of theatre, but when my agent rang to say I'd been offered a play there my heart sank because I had a small baby and had intended to take a year off. When I heard rehearsals were due to start in a week I immediately asked who had gone sick? Joan Plowright had been cast originally but she'd discovered she was pregnant and didn't fancy being buried in a hole all by herself at that time. I wasn't aware that Beckett had never seen Joan work – he'd liked her brown eyes and thought she could do the part. I didn't know the director, George

Devine, at all and it was only after we'd opened that he admitted he'd never seen me do anything and that John Dexter had suggested me.

When I read the play I was very irritated by all the lines of dots Beckett had put in between the words and I remember saying to my husband, "I do wish writers wouldn't do this, it's so constricting," and he said, "All that will get ironed out in rehearsals." Of course, when I started working with Beckett I found that the lines of dots were absolutely part of the play and that if I didn't attend to them on the split second I had to go right back to the beginning again. I realised what a nightmare it was going to be, not to have any chance to break down the script and learn it. If I'd had it even a month before, I could have got the worst of it out of the way, but as it was I had no time before Beckett was involved.

I was living in Brighton and Larry Olivier was a neighbour. He was rehearsing *Semi-Detached* at the time and we used to catch the same train at night and I told him about the difficulties I was having learning the play. He put his glasses on and said, "Give me the book, get out your powder compact and your lipstick and we'll go through it." So we went through *Happy Days* each evening on the Brighton Belle with the other passengers thinking we were completely nuts. It was very helpful to just keep going over and over it and I hoped it would finally become second nature. When I got home I would cook a meal and then get my husband to take me through the script again.

Beckett was at the rehearsals from the beginning, and whenever I asked him what something meant he would always say, " 'Tis of no consequence." I suppose I'd been rehearsing about a week, trying desperately to get off the book, when he came in with a metronome and set it off and said, "That's my rhythm." I just got absolutely hysterical. George Devine said to Sam, "I think you must leave us alone for a time. It's too much for her to have two people directing her at once." It wasn't that Beckett was being nasty to me, it was just that he didn't really understand how actors work.

Life was easier when I was working just with George but I wasn't suddenly allowed to do just what I wanted. He was very meticulous and always referred to Beckett and asked him, quite rightly, what he meant and wanted, but he was also very protective of me and I loved him.

I was aware that it was a tremendously important play and that in itself was scaring. I felt safe when Jocelyn was around and always thought she understood without her needing to say very much. She was so straight and there was no theatricality about her at all, she could see that the play was murderous and was very kind to me so I was at ease with her straight away. She and George lived in a studio with a wonderful atmosphere and I vividly remember the first time she asked me back there; I had imagined it would be rather chi-chi but it was quite the reverse. She cooked scrambled eggs and cauliflower and we ate at a long, scrubbed table. The way she lived had a huge effect on me and it's never worn off.

Beckett never saw *Happy Days* with an audience. He came in at the half on the first night with beautiful yellow roses and said, "Goodbye, my dear." I said, "You're not leaving me?" and he said, "Oh, yes," and away he went back to Paris. Jocelyn was marvellous that night. I was so nervous my hands were shaking too much to put my make-up on and the tears were just rolling down my face. She came in and said, "I really think you should have a brandy." My heart was hammering so hard that it hurt. Jocelyn took one arm and George the other, and they got me downstairs and then they put me in that mound and the stage manager came and shut it behind me and put the bolt in. It was dreadful. There was the claustrophobia of sitting there trapped, I couldn't ease it by walking across the stage. There I was with all those people looking at me, a great many of them thinking it rubbish – which they don't now. The physical and emotional horror aggravate one another. It is complete exposure because with the lighting there is no shadow anywhere, which is part of the play. You begin to get mesmerized by the lights.

Once *Happy Days* opened I was left to Jocelyn's tender mercies – George had gone off to lecture and Beckett was writing some more torture for somebody else. She would ring up at the half to see if I'd actually come in and she arrived herself almost every night. At every single performance there came a moment when I knew the audience couldn't take any more. I would phone Jocelyn in tears if people shouted or walked out. I remember telling Beckett that someone had shouted and finding he was delighted whereas, to me, it was mortifying.

I once asked Beckett, "Why did you write this play which is such a torture for me?" He said, "I asked myself the question: what would be the worst thing in the world? I thought, never to be allowed to sleep; to have blazing sun twenty four hours a day; not to be able to move; no shade of any kind; and a man you can't see and who is of no help whatsoever. And to have the means in sight to kill yourself and not the will to do it because inside you've always got that slight ray of hope." Then he said, "I thought, who would actually put up with that? Only a woman could." So he wrote it for a woman.

Happy Days haunted me and in the end I fell in love with it and toured South America with it, winning an award in Brazil. I don't know that I would want to do it again now, though.

Billie Whitelaw, actress

I first met Jocelyn when George Devine directed *Play* at the National Theatre, and I worked with her again on *Othello*. I took over the part of Desdemona from Maggie Smith and I remember Jocelyn's great care in remodelling the costumes and how she understood it was difficult to follow Maggie and never made me feel as if I was the second eleven. Without either of them needing to say a word, such love radiated between George and Jocelyn that I felt I could put my hand out and touch it. I think of my life as a series of snapshots and one image is of the two of them sitting down quietly at Maggie Smith's house after the first night of *Othello*; it was as if there was an umbrella of love all the way round them, and I bumshuffled over until I got nearer and nearer to them and hoped that some of their warmth would spill on to me. It did, and I have fed on that love for a long time.

Beckett adored both of them and, during *Play*, I became absolutely riveted by him. Another snapshot I've got in my mind is of Beckett sitting, with his scrubbing brush hair and his macintosh, in my dressing room at the Vic while we worked on the text. He sat in silence for about twenty minutes poring over two or three pages and I thought, "I must respect this silence, I mustn't interfere," and then he'd ask me to come over and bring a pencil and cross a little something out and I would know what he meant. Beckett doesn't write plays about things, he writes the thing itself. *Play* is not *about* a story, it *is* an event. I had enormous respect for Beckett but I wasn't frightened of him in the way I'd be frightened of a lot of other people; I felt safe with him. Jocelyn seemed to work by osmosis, she was so in tune with the text and she took enormous care.

Play was a lead up to *Not I*, which was the toughest theatre I've done. The first time I read it I wept buckets. I recognised the terror on the page. I wasn't crying for a seventy year old woman, I was crying because it struck something in me. I've been asked on television what the play is about and, on paper, it's the story of a woman who is seventy and keeps on saying she's sixty, and who goes into lavatories and has verbal diarrhoea, and who goes into supermarkets and tries to do her shopping. Having said that, one has said absolutely nothing. If *Not I* were about an old lady going crazy someone would have written a three act play, but Beckett has done the whole thing in sixteen minutes. To me it's an inner scream, like falling backwards into hell. At the time I did *Not I* my young son was recovering from a horrendous illness and that, to me, was what the play was about.

I knew what Beckett wanted, there was no argument and I agreed with him absolutely. Learning the text was the main problem and at that speed of delivery there's no time to collect your thoughts as to what comes next. I had certain signpost words – 'April', 'fields', 'Crocker's Acres' – and I could remember rhythms. My script looks as though a crazy centipede has crawled all over it. It seemed to me that the play was a series of broken sections and I used a system of colours to help me. Where a thought carried on for, perhaps, two sentences I would draw a balloon and colour it red to remind me to keep hold of it when I had to break and talk about something else. Then, lower down, when the thought came back I'd draw a little duck and colour it red as a signal that I had to pull down the balloon and attach it to the duck. When I was performing I would pull all these ropes in as I went along. It was like piloting a plane and each night I used to say to myself, "Pilot your own plane and ride the turbulences." It was an exercise in concentration and it never got easier.

I love *Happy Days*. When I first read it I rang Jocelyn and said, "How on earth could Sam write the story of my life twenty years before he knew me?" I recognise all his ladies. It took me three months to learn it and I shut myself away at the top of the house and learnt every comma, every semi-colon, every "ah, well", every "oh, yes". I drew the curtains and decided to have no night and no day, just twenty four hours. I had a tape machine, the text, pencils and paper, and I went over and over it aloud. I would emerge from time to time for food and then slither back upstairs like a creature. At the end of the three months my muscles had atrophied and I was like an old sack when I finally got out of the room – if you look at photographs of *Happy Days* you can see that my arms are all floppy. I did go slightly dotty and at that point I rang Brenda Bruce who said to me, "They'll tell you that if you can get through this, then you can get through anything. Well, I've never recovered."

After *Not I* the mound was freedom. There were little indentations which Jocelyn had made so that I could place the props very precisely where Sam wanted them. The set became my home. I've got hundreds of little china rabbits and I had about thirty of these underneath the mound so it was quite alive and very cosy. I didn't need a bar to hold onto because, to use Sam's word, I could 'recover' and in fact I would sometimes sit and stare into space just because I felt like it; I'd just think of nothing for a while and then start off again. By the time I did *Happy Days*, it was considered one of the more accessible of Sam's plays. Once I'd learnt it, it was a joy to do.

Beckett wrote *Footfalls* for me for his seventieth birthday. I never ask him what his plays are about because I can feel what's required and I'm not interested in what they're about. *Footfalls* was the only time I asked him anything about the work and I said, "Am I dead?" He thought for a minute and said, "Well, let's just say you're not quite there." I knew exactly what he meant, the strange no-man's land between life and death, consciousness and unconsciousness, grey, swirly air. I hadn't any idea what I should look like and knew I could leave it entirely to Jocelyn. The dress she made has been copied by many other people, but it's never looked the same. Like Topsy, it grew, it didn't seem to be stitched together. It felt like an organic thing that Jocelyn created rather than made and we seemed to have fertilizer sessions rather than fittings. I'd walk around in it a bit and Jos would tear a bit here and grab a bit there and so it grew.

Jocelyn's presence in rehearsals has always been tremendously important. She has such warmth. I've still got the plant which she gave me on the first night of *Not I*; it flowers every year with a lovely red bloom and I feel it's somehow part of her. I don't think she'll ever be the same without George, but it's as if she has absorbed his death and somehow come through it with even more love than before. Both she and Sam have integrity oozing out of every pore of them. There's nothing mini about either of them nor is there a malicious thought in either of their hearts or heads. What they have is a calm, still centre and I think they have got their values absolutely right.

Ronald Eyre, director

Jocelyn has a wonderful selective myopia or deafness and that used to puzzle me at first. She saves her own time and, probably, the life of the project by choosing not to engage when something comes up that doesn't seem to her to be useful. You think at first you're treading water. Then you realise somebody's taken the water away. After a time you begin to admire that ability as a wonderful, life-saving, time-saving way of being efficient. She's got great humour and she's very patient so you're allowed to flounder in her presence. She allows herself to flounder too.

You become different every time you work with a different designer, it's a bargain you strike each time. When Jocelyn's designing you know you're not going to get someone going on an ego trip. She is interested in the drama inside the play and not just in doing the packaging. She's always willing to talk about the play and goes on talking about it a long time after she's designed it. A lot of designers want to foreclose discussion and are extremely anxious to get past the bit where they talk with the director, whereas Jocelyn is most engaged at that moment and really wants to know what the text says to you. She doesn't bombard you with theories; she looks for the life and nurses it. Often there will be an element which she has quietly brought into the conversation or into the model which you don't notice is there and then you suddenly realise that it is the key to the design. She's wise enough to realise that anyone who says, "This is how it is," may please the management and get the design done quickly but they're possibly not hearing other voices in the play. It isn't that she's tentative, but she's always got an ear open for the tune she might have missed.

Jocelyn learnt from The Court that doing a production was a way of life; you plug yourself in like a dishwasher for the production's cycle and go through all the agonies together. Some designers don't want to get sucked into the production – they will service it and make it run and that's all. One sign of the decadence in a lot of the institutions I have brushed with in my time is that the continuous life of the company has become more important than the life of any one play. It means people are always slightly leaning into the future, either in the hope of future jobs or anticipating future fear. Jocelyn's life was much tied up with the continuity of The Court but I never felt with her that anything was more important at that moment than the play she was designing. She's interested in how the actors function and, for example, for *Three Months Gone*, which we did together, she fitted out a whole kitchen although it wasn't all seen by the audience. She knows that it isn't much help to ask someone to go out of a realish looking set into a place where there's a yawning member of the stage management standing in for an electric kettle.

The George Devine Award is a way of commemorating George and can be given to a designer or an actor but has, in fact, usually gone to writers. Jocelyn assembles a lively group of people and is wonderful at giving them their head and waiting for the squalls to blow themselves out. It's a very humane committee and she always finishes meetings by making a fantastic soup with chopped sausage and bread and wine. When it gets to voting time you're always relieved but in a way sad that the soup and the wine and the talk can't go on longer.

Peter Hall, director

I think two designers absolutely changed the course of British theatre design: one was Jocelyn and the other was John Bury. Before them most designers were encouraged to wrap up the pill with a lot of fancy paper but John and Jocelyn affected a whole generation of designers and directors and made them insist on the question, "It may be nice, but is it necessary?" John Bury began his career as an electrician in Joan Littlewood's Theatre Workshop whereas Jocelyn came at it as a painter. John believed in the real functioning of material and he dealt out the reality of texture, of soil and brickwork – his sets were less 'designed', less aesthetic than Jocelyn's. She removed everything from the stage that didn't fulfil a function and made something beautiful out of that minimalism.

I think her influence is very strong. It's an influence that takes me back to seeing the Berliner Ensemble in 1956 when they played in London, which had an enormous effect on all of us. Immediate post-war theatre had been sequinned and escapist, much more related to the world of ballet, a place of glamour, colour and fantasy. Suddenly there were plays dealing with what it was like to be alive at that moment and I think Jocelyn was terribly excited by that new generation of writers; she cared about their plays, she cared about what they were saying and the designs grew out of that. The effect of it at the time was as if somebody had taken a really good cleansing fluid and washed all the varnish off so you could see the picture. Jocelyn and her school made everybody realise that a plain wooden bowl on stage could be beautiful – it didn't have to be decorated – and that was quite staggering, a breath of fresh air.

She made something very beautiful out of minimalism. At her best I don't think her minimalism is ever arid or dry or abstract because what there is can be breathtakingly beautiful and very colourful. She doesn't eschew colour but it has to be used with real meaning, not for effect. There is something puritanical about her minimalism, but it's passionate, very strong and not at all repressed. Sometimes I've felt she carried minimalism to a point where it was almost too modest, and that would be the most I would fault her for. I've never seen anything of hers which has been over-designed or over-decorated. She's a very strong lady and has a firm vision of what she's about. She knows who she is artistically, and that's what strength is. Her relationship with George Devine was a wonderfully creative marriage and together they developed what Michel Saint-Denis had taught and preached. I was taught by Michel at a slightly later stage because he was with me in the early years of the RSC, so I feel we all stem in some way from Michel. There was a lot you could take from him, all of us in our different ways; Michel was a very rich man in that sense.

I've spent nearly thirty years of my life employing directors and working with them and many times they will say, "I'll do the play if Jocelyn is free to design it." She almost never is free because she doesn't like to overload herself; sometimes I can persuade the director to work with someone else but I honestly can't think of any other designer that directors say that about so often. The great people who have clear handwriting all have imitators and Jocelyn inevitably does. I think her influence has made the designer's craft more intellectually challenging. Too many designers expected a director to give them a groundplan of roughly what they wanted and they would then do a beautiful sketch and someone else would make the model. Jocelyn has always worked with models, thinking in the third dimension, believing that theatre design is a three-dimensional business, which it assuredly is. Her talent has altered the expectation of what a designer should be and what he has to aspire to.

I asked Jocelyn to do *The Oresteia* because I wanted someone who was prepared and would be excited to explore the world of the mask. I always feel that the Greek stage is itself a mask because the pain and the action and the screaming and the murder happen behind closed doors. I thought Jocelyn would be superb at giving me a strong neutrality to the set. What was wonderful about her work on *The Oresteia* was that she set about it in a very humble way and started with nothing, no solutions. She went on a long journey to find how those masks should be and how they should work, that's why it took months and months. It's a painstaking, long and difficult process of trial and error, all the time judging every solution you come to in the most ruthless way, and Jocelyn has a great capacity for that; she knows immediately if something's wrong or right.

A full mask in Greek tragedy must laugh when the sound of laughter is heard and it must cry when the sound of sobbing is heard. If the mask itself lacks that ambiguity it will push you towards a fixed emotion which you can't escape from; it has to express the character of the individual but yet be able to change expression. What a mask does on one person, it doesn't do on another: the masks of the Old Men became many different things as the emotion was expressed.

Actors, of course, resist the mask. If what you sell and what you communicate with is your identity, then your face is the primary part of that, and for someone to come along and say, "I don't like your face, here's another one," is a terrible imposition. Several actors we had on *The Oresteia* found it impossible, one practically had a nervous breakdown and got sick. If you really do proper mask work, it confronts the actor with himself in the most inexorable way; if you lie as an actor, if you have falseness in you, the mask will tell you that you do. It's a terrible thing for an actor to face. Once you accept the mask and what the mask does to you, then it's extraordinarily liberating.

Of all the things I've done, *The Oresteia* was one of the most dangerous and difficult journeys I've been on. Jocelyn's collaborative work was crucial. When we played at Epidaurus, I felt a vindication of our work, it seemed as if it had come home and had really communicated and succeeded.

David Reppa, Resident Designer at the Metropolitan Opera, New York, since 1966

The first thing that one notices about Jocelyn is her tremendous enthusiasm. Her freshness of approach is rare, it's almost as if she's doing her first production and yet you know there are years and years of accumulated experience and problem solving behind her. We, unfortunately, get some designers at the Met who have done the same production elsewhere and are not that interested, so they will leave a lot of the designer's work and the problem solving to us. We've always got productions from Jocelyn that are finished when they arrive here – in other words she and John Dexter have worked out the problems in advance. She does her homework and brings in a lot of research so that we can get the clearest possible picture of what she wants.

Jocelyn has always found the solution to the Met's space in her own way, not relying too much on the equipment of the theatre. Designing is very often not what you put in but what you leave out. She's one of the greatest designers I know and will always stand up to a director if she feels something is right, whereas most designers will back down. One quality that I envy in her is her self-assurance; she knows what she wants and she knows how to get it diplomatically. She's more open to suggestions than a lot of designers, as assured people always are – it's the people who are very nervous and insecure who never let you change anything. If the concept of the design is terrific, changing one little detail here or there isn't going to make a difference.

Jocelyn is one of those people who never alters; she's not a different person in rehearsal than she is when you're sitting having lunch. There's a lot of affection for her here simply because she was interested in us so we, in turn, became interested in her and her work. It's not unusual for a designer never to go round and thank the people in the workshops after they've been here, but Jocelyn is not like that at all. She'll sit down and eat with the workshops' crew and not talk about herself or the work, but will listen to their problems instead.

I think she doesn't get involved in small issues and she knows what really counts in the long run – that's true of her work and her life – and a lot of us don't have that quality or knowledge. She's unique in the theatre and she's unique as a person. When she and John were at the Met a lot of opera clichés vanished; some people liked it and some didn't, but I think the two of them are sorely missed.

Lulu was a refreshing surprise to most of us because it was totally different from what we were used to seeing. It's one of the operas you either love or you hate, there's no middle ground. Jocelyn opted for trucks to make the production dramatically more exciting. Her use of the double wagons for scene shifting was almost totally contrary to the way the theatre works – the Met works with a lift system and a fly system. All the open scene changes the audience usually sees are done parallel to the footlights or perpendicular to them, but Jocelyn's wagons came out from the wings on the diagonal at a forty five degree angle. One of the big problems of opera is waiting for the scene changes and *Lulu*, especially, requires continuous action, so Jocelyn's solution worked beautifully because it was a system where the changes could be made quickly and completely. Also, by using the wagons, she contained the action within a given space and was able to work with the small interiors which this opera needs. The only departure from that was the one large scene in the opera (the gambling scene) when the floor itself was used, with hanging pieces flown in.

The drapes in *Lulu* were flown in hanging from pelmets and dropped right into place. The curtains for Schön's room were very, very heavy and made from rather inexpensive material, sprayed and dyed. The scale in the design of the fabric was unusual for us and rather large, so the only way we could do it was to lay the fabric out and paint it. In the dressing room scene, the walls were red flock wallpaper and looked like red velvet. That, again, was unusual for us, almost like a television technique. With the combination of drapes and wagons, Jocelyn set a small cast opera in a confined acting area, using only a very small part of the stage without the audience being aware of it; it's very hard to achieve that and, in fact, this production worked very well when it was telecast.

Mahagonny was a real departure for the Met. It was very exciting for us, we always like change here because we do the standard operas again and again, and it's a challenge to have a new work that you don't know all about and for which you have to find the answers. John Dexter and Jocelyn were the perfect people to do it. Someone unfamiliar with Brecht could never have come up with a design like Jocelyn's, and it worked very well because she had a concept for the whole opera.

One of the biggest problems was that it had a wooden floor and, because the opera is played in repertory, we had to put down all the planks between three in the afternoon and eight in the evening, so it was always a race to get it done in time. Fortunately, the rest of the production was on the light side so there was very little scenery to be prepared. Another problem was stretching the curtain from one side of the stage to the other on a cable. The curtain must have been around forty eight feet long and it had to reach offstage without sagging in the middle, so we had a very fine wire holding it in the centre. It was a very Brechtian curtain, pulled across by hand, and short so the audience upstairs could see right over the top of it – we'd never had anything like that on the stage at the Met before.

Another part of Jocelyn's enthusiasm is that she's interested in materials that aren't traditionally used in theatre. I'm never surprised by anything designers want because we're like crows and if we see something shiny – anything we think we can use – we grab onto it. During *Mahagonny*, Jocelyn and I were wandering around the area near Canal Street and she caught sight of some iridescent reflective paper which we bought and used for the signs. Other designers will go shopping but if what they see is inexpensive then they're not interested, but Jocelyn isn't like that at all and I remember when we shopped for *Lulu* ninety five percent of the furniture was purchased from antique or junk shops.

One aspect of *Mahagonny* wasn't right and I think it was our fault. There were supposed to be clouds going by with writing on them for one of the scenes and somehow that never got worked out technically and the problem was never solved. It can be very difficult in an organization of this size when someone has an idea and that idea is handed on to someone else and gets slightly changed and handed on again – like Chinese whispers.

Simon Usher, director

I worked with Jocelyn on what was, in a sense, her introduction to a 'fringe' production, and I was nervous of asking her to work with such a low budget and small cast. We had to find a way to do *Timon of Athens* in a studio theatre without making the play small. Our notion was to produce an epic in miniature. I think we both felt the play was operatic in some senses, the second half of the play is one big aria with interventions from different characters in a different key.

I had particularly loved Jocelyn's design for *The Devil and the Good Lord* because of its sculptural quality, and that was the production I had in mind when we started talking, but I didn't find it easy to say that to her because it might have sounded as if I just wanted her to do something she'd done before. I started out with all kinds of ideas that I didn't think were very good, almost encouraging her to knock them down and get back to basics. We talked about various different settings, but quite half-heartedly, until one day we finally got down to the nitty-gritty; I said I would need some door-frames and she leapt at that.

What I liked best about working with Jocelyn was that we were talking about what was going to happen on stage right from the beginning, we were focused on the movement and the pattern of the whole play before we began talking about what kind of archways we would have or what colour they would be. We talked about particular speeches in the play quite a bit and in our first conversations I think we disagreed about how to read the play, and I'm not sure that we agree on it now, but it turned out not to matter because she believes in letting the text live and so do I. One thing that we both loved was that the piece is unique in Shakespeare's work in its versification and the rapid movement between verse and prose; you have six lines of irregular verse and then a paragraph of prose and then four rhyming couplets at the end of that. We both felt that was where the life of the play resided.

Jocelyn said that she thought Timon should be physically at the centre of the action and that the other characters should revolve round him in a kind of orbit like a chorus. From there we went to talking about the play as a sort of epic with token characters, half-realised people. Even Timon is not a fully-fledged character with a fulfilled psychology but, rather, a big fragment in the play whilst the other characters are relatively smaller fragments. In a sense the language of the play passes through them rather than their creating it.

Jocelyn contributes much more than other designers I've worked with, and I loved it. Very often with designers you have to do the work for them or tell them in minute details, but with her it was a much more suggestive relationship. Her design for *Timon* was very coherent, considered and economical; as she says, doing the play as the author wants is actually a more creative discipline than coming up with an interpretation. I think the bane of the theatre today is the business of making sets as statements because that kind of articulateness about what's going to happen in a play can be very reductive and damaging.

The *Timon* company had never worked with anyone as rigorous or as attentive to detail as Jocelyn. One of her great characteristics is that she never shirks anything that needs to be said. When an actor grumbles about costume or details, she will argue in the context of the whole production in a convincing way. She's also very good with people and never makes anyone feel less important than anyone else, so I found her a very serene influence on everyone. Her presence calms people down and concentrates their energies well. She takes her work very seriously but there isn't any puritanism there, which is very refreshing these days when you have to listen to so much earnestness all the time.

David Gothard, artistic associate at the Haymarket Theatre, Leicester, at the time of interview

Jocelyn's genius expresses itself in moments which other people might think were just banal or chance. An example was the way she conjured up a whole army in *Timon of Athens* when the entire cast was only seven people. The army was portrayed by just two actors and a flag. She used the flag to give the audience a beautiful, Brechtian image which depended precisely on the way in which the flag was held and how it moved. The flow of the flag was sensual in the way that a ballet movement is sensual and at the same time it evoked something epic. She is, of course, devoted to her friend, the great choreographer, Merce Cunningham.

I first worked with Jocelyn on the Beckett triple bill at the Theatre Upstairs. I learnt the kind of details that often seem dull but which in fact you only get from the best people and you never, ever forget them. You can spend the rest of your life going through the theatre and never finding that level of care and attention again, so you'd better remember it. In *Come and Go*, the breeze that moved the ladies' veils and the plumes on their hats was terribly important to the design. Jocelyn spent a great deal of time and care with the technician to get that just right, to achieve the right emotional frisson. She's always very practical but also aesthetically humanist. She can conjure up something very simple and artistically very powerful without it being a symbol. The other thing I remember is the amount of time I spent handing her tacks. I'd used staples to fix the blacks to the rostra and she said it had to be done with tacks so they didn't catch the light.

Jocelyn is very English at a time when it's difficult to talk about Englishness. With her, you feel that for a brief period you are living and working in an important way and that has become very rare in the theatre. She represents a vital point of reference in the theatre culture, but she's no mere saint – no artist is.

David Leveaux, director

Jocelyn is one of the most sensual designers working on the English stage. She finds lyricism in austerity. The empty landscapes of our really great modern artists are filled with vivid and colourful ghosts of history, and that is why their spaces are so lively; Jocelyn has the ability to find a point in space and a point in a play to create the maximum dynamism which is why her reductive work is so energetic. She can show the whole of the nineteenth century in the line of a tree. She understands where to find the spring of beauty and has the knack of putting that on stage.

It's not accidental that Jocelyn has a powerful relationship with Beckett. The reason why his plays are short is exactly the same reason that her sets are minimal. It's like Beckett's directions for a character to sing a song: no song comes, yet you hear it.

Hayden Griffin, designer

I grew up in South Africa, trained as a commercial artist and got into theatre design by accident. I didn't come to live in England until I was twenty, so although I knew of Jocelyn's work, I didn't know an awful lot about it. I first met her when I was at the Sadler's Wells Design School and, although she wasn't on the staff, Percy [Margaret Harris] got her in to do a project with us.

I found her enormously formidable and she was very tough and heavy about anything I did. There were eight students in my year and she took a particular dislike to my work and hammered away at me, making me realise that I'd been floating all over the place. The great thing about her constant carping was that she opened a floodgate and forced me to understand that you can't impose a design on a piece of work, that you must study the text and get the instinct for the visual feel of the play from that. She unlocked my ability to analyse a play and from then on I have applied that knowledge to everything I do.

The project we were doing was *The Tempest* and, although I remember her liking the costumes, her final analysis of my design was that I'd put a great lump in the middle of the stage and that the actors couldn't move on the set. I have never made that mistake again, and ever after I've always made sure that the acting space is usable by actors. I'm always very critical of designers who don't do this.

Even so, Jocelyn must have thought I'd coped all right with *The Tempest* because after that, without warning, I started getting phone calls from people saying that they'd asked Jocelyn to design for them but since she wasn't available she'd recommended me. It went on for about ten years and, although I don't know her very well as a person, my first really important jobs came through Jocelyn.

She taught me (and, I think, the whole of my generation of designers) by example rather than through formal teaching. She is the greatest exponent of creating the design from the script, therefore her work has a vibrancy; nothing she does on stage detracts from the play. Another lesson I absorbed from her was her great belief in working on new material, and it was my work on many new plays which made it easier for me to design plays from the past. Now I approach Shakespeare or other period writers in the same way as I approach a new work, as if it's never been seen before.

Jocelyn never gets the space wrong. She led me to understand that you can't ignore the architecture of the building you're designing in. A lot of designers work behind an imaginary black frame, as if they're doing a picture and what they do exists only within that border, but Jocelyn never does that. Her use of The Royal Court showed that she understood that theatre inside out. One of the first things she did there was to make sure the auditorium and the stage tied together – which is what makes it feel so intimate – and she achieved it simply by painting it all the same shade of brown.

Jocelyn tells me she goes through the same hell with every new project, believing she hasn't got any ideas, thinking she's never going to solve the problems and won't be able to make it refreshing and exciting to an audience. She always says that she can't draw very well, which is rubbish. She and Caspar Neher have done the best theatre drawings I've ever seen, and, although it's not her intention, her drawings are always beautiful in themselves. She'll do a lot of drawings where she does groups of characters to illustrate a scene – like Neher, her characters are very much of the texture of the play she's working on. You get a very strong, deep feeling of the period or world of the play but at the same time her costumes look like inventions, something you've never seen before. That's why she's a marvellous designer and stands out among the people who simply re-create the period on stage so that the costumes look as if they came out of books.

Out of her drawings emerges the blocking for the play. She completely influences the way a production grows and I'm certain that's why people like Lindsay Anderson and John Dexter insist on using her because they know they're going to get enormous back-up and won't be working on the play by themselves. She's very tough and I've never seen her do something which somebody else has suggested but of which she disapproved. I know by report that she's had enormous rows with Anderson and Dexter, but I'm sure she always quietly gets her own way. I do the same job and I know how tough you have to be. I've sometimes refused to do things because I didn't think they were right but then I've often not worked with the director concerned again; Jocelyn manages to avoid that, which means she must be incredibly strong to get through without breaking up the working relationship.

What stands out for me among all Jocelyn's work is the Mozart opera, *Die Entführung aus dem Serail*, which she did at the Met. It was staggering because she'd gone for a celebration of pure colour. It was a wonderfully staged piece and she managed to make a chamber opera intimate in a 5,000 seat house by building a thrust over the orchestra pit so that the piece seemed to be presented on the audience's lap. The workshops at the Met loved her; she just gets on with everyone and knows how to handle people, which is one of the reasons she gets great results.

I didn't think *The Mask of Orpheus* was that marvellous, but I can't lay the blame at Jocelyn's door. Also, it was very lazily and badly lit. I've worked in the same building and know what battles Jocelyn must have had to get co-operation from the workshops. The dyeing of the cloth she used for the river scene was very unlike Jocelyn and not properly done. The other thing I remember is that the Greek tunics looked out of style, which again seemed unlike her. I think she got the Greek character in her chorus costumes for *Orpheus and Euridice* at Sadler's Wells in 1967 much better than in *The Mask of Orpheus*; they were totally simple and had very strong straight and diagonal lines. *Orpheus and Euridice* was wonderfully designed, one of the most beautiful pieces of her work that I've ever seen.

Her influence has filtered through in various ways. I remember her *Woman Killed With Kindness*, which was done very simply on a platform but there was so much colour in the costumes that you remember it as a huge, colourful production. It had a dark 'box' surround and that surround was used by Bill Gaskill to influence Christopher Moreley when they did the Scottish play at The Royal Court. From there the 'box' travelled to Stratford with Christopher Moreley's designs so it's an example of the progression of one particular design solution through the theatre.

Jocelyn is the one designer working today who genuinely believes in theatre magic. Theatre magic is not necessarily the scale of *The Phantom of the Opera* nor is it the most wonderful aria in the world; it's producing an electricity in the audience when something happens – a line is understood or an action is placed so beautifully on stage that you know the whole audience is taking in their breath. If you get the actor in the right position at the right time (and that's most probably to do with having built up a series of images leading to that moment) then you get a magic ingredient which you cannot achieve simply by big, flamboyant theatre. Often these very, very beautiful, simple-looking productions can be more expensive than the extravagant-seeming ones: it can cost more money to get it right than to just cover the stage with decoration.

Tony Harrison, poet, playwright and director

My experience of working with Jocelyn has been very formative for me. We have worked together in the area of Greek drama, either in adaptations of the Greek or in new pieces based on ancient subjects: The National Theatre *Oresteia*, *The Trackers of Oxyrhynchus*, the as yet unrealised *The Common Chorus* (a combination of the *Lysistrata* of Aristophanes and *The Trojan Women* of Euripides set at Greenham Common) and what I call a 'sex war opera', *Medea*, commissioned by the Metropolitan Opera in New York and abandoned when the composer didn't deliver the music. Most recently we have worked on *Square Rounds* in 1992.

The reason I am drawn to Greek theatre is that, first and foremost, it was one which believed in the primacy of the word. What Jocelyn brings to this work is an enormous faith in writing as a theatrical power, as the main dynamo, bringing the tradition of commitment to the contemporary writer developed at The Royal Court into the arena of ancient Greek drama. That commitment is a marvellous tool for discovering the contemporaneity of an ancient piece. Even when I feel discouraged it is Jocelyn, paradoxically, as the designer who reminds me to trust in the text. As you know, it's quite common in modern theatre to do everything else but trust the text, and this lack of faith shows in much design and production. In this atmosphere a poet can feel overpowered and diminished by other elements of a production. This is never the case with Jocelyn. A poet could be blessed with no better theatrical collaborator.

People who write about the drama of ancient Greece but have no practical experience of theatre often assume that because the text is rich the production must have been correspondingly lavish. Jocelyn's commitment to writing gives her an understanding that Greek theatre created its strongest effects by *not* illustrating the text. She is the perfect designer to unlock that basic fact of Greek theatre.

When we worked on *The Oresteia* Jocelyn was central to the vision of what a masked drama might have been like. Her designs are not self-effacing, the elements are very striking and often have a bold simplicity which makes a very strong effect, but at the same time creates a space and a visual focus in which the text can work its spell. *The Oresteia* was a long journey and we made many discoveries together. She was the one who knew most about masks, and she taught us all that the mask learns from the language it has to speak and not from gazing into mirrors. She prevented people from generalising about 'masks'. She was very careful to distinguish between the masks of, say, *commedia dell'arte* and the classic Greek mask which was created to make its effects where language is the main stirrer of the imagination.

Susan Harris Smith in her book, *Masks in Modern Drama* (which has, like so many books on the mask, Jocelyn's Furies on the cover) says that "the mask challenges the primacy of language..." This is the kind of generalisation (which I think, by the way, is one hundred percent wrong) that Jocelyn would never allow. I think the exciting discovery was for me that the mask reinforced the primacy of language, that the classical mask of fifth century Athenian theatre was an existential device to carry tragic meaning and survival, and allow speech to continue in situations that might render us otherwise speechless. This, for me, was a profound discovery and could not have been made without Jocelyn's guidance and experience. My interest in this ancient theatre was part of a search for a style with which to speak about our own times. There was never at any time any question of 'antique reproduction' and if there had been, from any quarter in the *Oresteia* production, Jocelyn would have been the first to challenge it.

My part in *The Oresteia* workshops was to discover what kind of language might it have been that worked when spoken in a mask in a large open-air theatre. Greek texts have a built-in performability and energy to enable them to spellbind their audiences in those conditions. I tried to avoid the, to me, precious and 'melodious' style of translation because I associated it with worn out traditions of English acting and English culture. This rejection, though, could have practical support also when we discovered, for example, that the lengthened vowels of this rather self-regarding style of acting actually made the masks vibrate and the sound became mushy. I opted for a consonantal, alliterative energy with short Northern vowels.

It often seemed to me that Jocelyn and I were tunnelling from different ends but towards the same goal. The masks she created did not have their features distorted by the passions they were supposed to be feeling. They had a beautiful neutrality until, that is, they were worn by the actor and became animated by the emotions expressed by means of the text.

Another example is the discovery we made about what is called *stichomythia* in Greek tragedy, formally matched pairs of question and answer which are at the heart of the plays and have a great bearing on the use of masks and also the style of the language. Jocelyn helped me to understand that the two were inseparably related. Actors tend to look on these exchanges as a bit of 'real' dialogue and their instinct is to play them naturalistically. It doesn't work like that. (In masks the intimate tête-à-tête is in any case prevented by the way the mask turns all performance towards the audience.) What we discovered was that the *stichomythia* represented a kind of formal 'gear-change' in which the mask could have its emotion turned from one colour to another. For example, the Herald in the *Agamemnon* wears the same mask and has to come on and give first the speech of victory and elation and then give the bad news. The way he moves from the victorious and triumphant to the sad and defeated is through the *stichomythia*.

We would never have made this discovery about the formal change of these lines without masks, but they had to be the kind of masks that only someone as committed to language as Jocelyn could have created. You can just imagine how excited I was about such discoveries when you read scholars trying to work out how masks were changed from scene to scene to express new emotions, and that new entrances had to have new angers or fears etched into the mask's features. Thankfully, Jocelyn made us realise that the etching was done by the text.

In earlier *Oresteia* workshops, before Jocelyn was involved, those actors who were participating were issued with rather appalling, grotesque masks. After all, I suppose the thinking was, they are described as dripping with blood and snot. Jocelyn found that the ancient vases showed the Furies as rather beautiful so that, again, the main responsibility for their hideousness was carried by the poetic description of the terrified priest or the guilt-ridden conscience of Orestes. Similarly, I remember there was a discussion about the emergence of the tableau of the dead Agamemnon and Cassandra on the wheeled truck that the Greeks called the *ekkyklema*. Clytemnestra stands behind her victims in gloating triumph. The director wanted a lot of 'blood' but Jocelyn resisted this and what she came up with was a single silk glove, the domestication of blood, which was linked to the red cloth that rolled out to welcome Agamemnon back from Troy and to the cloaks given to the Furies as a token of their acceptance into the community at the very end of the trilogy. Jocelyn will stand up for these stylistic values when other people are losing faith in the text. And when these 'other people' have included me, the poet in the depths of self-doubt, I have to bless Jocelyn for restoring my faith by her single-minded commitment.

As well as *The Oresteia* we have worked on *The Trackers of Oxyrhynchus* originally intended for one unique performance at the ancient Stadium of Delphi in July 1988. And we have had long conversations about a production for The Olivier of the *Lysistrata* and *The Trojan Women*. I believe that the best theatre is written for a space that the writer knows. When I create a piece I always imagine the space in which it is going to be played. Jocelyn will explain to me the possible physical capabilities of a space, whether it is The Olivier at the NT, which I think she has a unique understanding of, or the huge ancient Stadium of Delphi. In the case of the Delphi Stadium we explored its physical potential some time before I started work on the play. In fact, we made three trips there, once when we both spoke about masks at the Delphi Symposium, and twice to prepare for *The Trackers of Oxyrhynchus*. Our conversations there were very important to me. And I don't mean simply about the Stadium, or even about the theatre for that matter. Jocelyn's spirit is very positive and she has a real rapport with Greece. It's important to me to go on exploring the Greek repertory and to go on exploring it with Jocelyn because we carry our discoveries from piece to piece. They are deep discoveries and not the kind I could give to some new designer because they come out of Jocelyn's lifetime's faith in a certain type of theatre and style which draws its energy from the text. For me, for the poet that I am, with the theatrical obsessions that I have, all I can say is that I met the right person at the right time, someone who has constantly been able to give me back my often wavering faith in language.

Although *The Trackers of Oxyrhynchus* had been planned for one performance, it was later rewritten and rethought for The Olivier Theatre in March 1990. We also played at Salt's Mill, Saltaire, and in the grounds of Schloss Petronell at Carnuntum on the Austrian/Slovak border. It had another run in The Olivier from February 1991 and toured to Odense and the Gasworks Theatre in Copenhagen and to the Brighton Festival. Adapting the piece to The Olivier was a real pleasure as both Jocelyn and I love a space that sometimes scares others by its openness. In all the other venues, I rewrote and Jocelyn was there not only to supervise how our desert should look in each new place, but also painting, sawing, sewing, sometimes up to the last minute. I have many fond images of her in these situations from as early as *The Oresteia* when I arrived at the ancient theatre of Epidaurus to find her up a ladder adding the last daubs to the palace of Atreus before the performance that evening. Or up a very shaky, windblown ladder rehanging the papyrus strips ripped and torn off their posts by the storm that wrecked our set and technical rehearsals at Delphi; sewing furiously on a Singer under the shades of fig and olive in temperatures of over one hundred degrees; on her knees repainting the desert floor of *Trackers* at Salt's Mill and making the fixed pillars of the weaving sheds into the broken columns of some long buried temple at Oxyrhynchus; in the Schloss Petronell on the Danube, again on her knees, repainting the desert floor after an April hailstorm had ruined the floorcloth; again, extending the desert in Odense, always ready with a practical hand to give vision the substance and detail it needs to become theatre.

The thought we had both given to the now abandoned combined trilogy of *Lysistrata*, *The Trojan Women* and a new piece about the invention of the machine gun and chemical weapons, helped us to rethink *Trackers* for The Olivier, and also made us want to create another piece for that space after *Trackers* had finished its limited run. The Greenham Common setting for the abandoned trilogy had become somewhat historically marooned by the end of the Cold War, but the third part of it came back to me during the anxieties and horrors of the Gulf War. One of the themes of the play had been how the invention of the machine gun created the deadlock of trench warfare which needed some new weapon to break it, and this led to the introduction into the world arsenal of chemical weapons and of the first use of chlorine gas. There was much discussion and much hypocrisy on the subject during the Gulf War and I resolved to finish what became *Square Rounds*, which opened in The Olivier on

1 October 1992. It was also to be about the redemptive possibilities of the human imagination, and the precarious balance between creation and destruction.

I had been thinking about the piece and collecting material for about twenty years and as with any long and layered project it needed a bold simplification to resolve its tensions and contradictions. There is no-one better to talk to at this stage, before even the workshop text has been written, than Jocelyn. She has an ability to share a vision without making it conventional but at the same time finding physical images to earth the lightning. She was extraordinarily patient with my crude sketches and kindergarten collages. I bombarded her with images of men in top hats; the gentleman 'inventor' removed from the bloody action he contributes to; the conjuror producing silks from it; the formal funeral director; Vesta Tilley; Burlington Bertie. What resulted was a beautifully formal black circle on a white floor, with three screens on which were projected images of blasted trees which could have been from the shell-shattered landscapes of the First World War or from the acid-rain wasted landscapes of polluted Europe. I thought she made The Olivier look as beautiful as it had ever looked. Whatever else it was, I believe that *Square Rounds* produced one of the best designs Jocelyn had ever done.

After long periods of despair about finding a style, we had workshops which involved Jocelyn with the magician Ali Bongo and Arturo Bracchetti, the Italian quick-change genius. She warmed to their inventiveness and painstaking practicality, which she recognised as close to her own, and the style of *Square Rounds* emerged from the month in The NT studio and long subsequent sessions at her own studio before the beautiful model that she always makes for a production. I loved these visits to Princedale Road, sitting for hours with a glass of her favourite Pouilly Fumé or retsina, moving the cut-out figures stabilised with blobs of plasticine about the modelled Olivier stage. Even before the text was finalised this process helped me to clarify the quite complicated things I wanted to explore. It was for me a deeply important process because behind it I detected, in both designer and poet, a need to make (or remake) the theatrical process more organic, to rescue actor and text from the suffocation of naturalism or from being dwarfed by high-tec. I felt in those sessions that it was possible to create a new poetic theatre, that drew from the past, but which looked straight into the depths and disturbance of our times.

There were two 'eureka' moments on *Square Rounds* that I celebrate. One was when we were both poring over albums of pictures in The Imperial War Museum and, from an album of improvised gas alarms made out of old iron and oil drums, we hit upon the idea of the gas attack at the front being changed by these means into a Chinese orchestra taking us from the First World War back to ancient China where all the weapons boasted of by their Western inventors – guns, chemical projectiles – had been thought of centuries ago. And the second was very late after a long session in Jocelyn's studio with the model, going through scenes over and over, when she put up the scene where the invention of gas for use as mass-destruction is represented by beautifully coloured silks falling over the black circle in succession. These suddenly beautiful silks produced from the 'top hat' were paradoxically the poisonously lethal gases from chlorine to Zyklon B, and they would hang there until Arturo Bracchetti, as the Chinese conjuror, would redeem them in the costumes worn by the Chinese Dancers. It had the qualities I had hoped for, that I'd seen in my mind's eye but couldn't see before my very eyes until Jocelyn's vision and practical patience had given it substance. I was very moved by what I saw because I also knew that it was inspired by the Matisse of the late collages, an artist we both adored.

I often suffered from self-doubt over the difficulties of this piece, and although Jocelyn often disagreed with me over details which she was vigorously opposed to, she was never once unsupportive and I have never known her to be negative. If I had nothing else to be grateful to her for, and I have more than I could ever give words to, then I will never forget her loyalty, both artistic and personal, during this very ambitious enterprise, when many people around us were losing faith. What was remarkable, I remember thinking once, though after all I have known of her I shouldn't have been surprised, was that the oldest member of the company was also the most adventurous spirit in the room.

I can't wait to start on our next collaboration!

Cast lists

The Good Woman of Setzuan
by Bertolt Brecht
(translated by Eric Bentley)
31 October 1956
The Royal Court Theatre.

Wang:	Peter Woodthorpe
1st God:	Esme Percy
2nd God:	John Moffatt
3rd God:	Robert Stephens
Shen Te:	Peggy Ashcroft
Mrs Shin:	Joan Plowright
Wife:	Sheila Ballantine
Husband:	John Nettleton
Nephew:	Stephen Dartnell
Brother:	Michael Murray
Sister-in-law:	Jill Showell
Boy:	Frazer Hines
Grandfather:	John Rae
Niece:	Maureen Quinney
Unemployed Man:	Colin Jeavons
Lin To:	John Osborne
Mrs Mi Tzu:	Rachel Kempson
Policeman:	Nigel Davenport
Mrs Ma:	Lilian Moubrey
Yang Sun:	Peter Moubrey
Old Prostitute:	Margery Caldicott
Mr Shu Fu:	George Devine
Mr Ma:	Robert Gillespie
Mrs Yang:	Golda Casimir
Priest:	Michael Murray
Waiter:	Sean Kelly
Feng:	Norman Foreman
Carpenter's Other Son:	Maurice Bennis
Director:	George Devine
Design:	Teo Otto

The Chairs
by Eugene Ionesco
14 May 1957
The Royal Court Theatre.

The Old Man:	George Devine
The Old Woman:	Joan Plowright
The Orator:	Richard Pasco
Director:	Tony Richardson
Music:	John Addison

Purgatory
by W.B. Yeats
22 July 1957
The Devon Festival.

Old Man:	John Phillips
Boy:	Graham James
Director:	John Dexter

The Sport of My Mad Mother
by Ann Jellicoe
25 February 1958
The Royal Court Theatre.

Flim (Steve):	Anthony Valentine
Caldaro (Dean):	Jerry Stovin
Patty:	Sheila Ballantine
Fak:	Philip Locke
Cone:	Paul Bailey
Dodo:	Avril Elgar
Greta:	Wendy Craig
Directors:	George Devine & Ann Jellicoe

The Lesson
by Eugene Ionesco
18 June 1958
The Royal Court Theatre.

The Professor:	Edgar Wreford
The Girl Pupil:	Joan Plowright
The Maid:	Phyllis Morris
Director:	Tony Richardson

Krapp's Last Tape
by Samuel Beckett
28 October 1958
The Royal Court Theatre.

Krapp:	Patrick Magee
Directors:	George Devine & Donald McWhinnie

Endgame
by Samuel Beckett
28 October 1958
The Royal Court Theatre.

Hamm:	George Devine
Clov:	Jack MacGowran
Nagg:	Richard Goolden
Nell:	Frances Cuka
Directors:	George Devine & Donald McWhinnie

Roots
by Arnold Wesker
25 May 1959
The Belgrade Theatre, Coventry, transferring to The Royal Court Theatre 30 June 1959 and to the Duke of York's Theatre 30 July 1959.

Jenny Beales:	Patsy Byrne
Jimmy Beales:	Charles Kay
Beatie Bryant:	Joan Plowright
Stan Mann:	Patrick O'Connell
Mrs Bryant:	Gwen Nelson
Mr Bryant:	Jack Rodney
Mr Healey:	Richard Martin
Frankie Bryant:	Alan Howard
Pearl Bryant:	Brenda Peters
Director:	John Dexter

The Kitchen
by Arnold Wesker
13 September 1959
The Royal Court Theatre.

Magi:	Alan Howard
First Waitress:	Jennifer Wallace
Max:	Tenniel Evans
Mangolis:	Peter Gill
Paul:	Alfred Lynch
Raymond:	James Culliford
Anne:	Patsy Byrne
Second Waitress:	Tarn Bassett
Third Waitress:	Mary Miller
Fourth Waitress:	Jeanne Watts
Dimitri:	Charles Kay
Hans:	Christopher Sandford
Alfredo:	Jack Rodney
Gaston:	David Ryder
Michael:	James Bolam
Bertha:	Gwen Nelson
Nicholas:	Anthony Carrick
Kevin:	John Briggs
Peter:	Robert Stephens
Frank, Second Chef:	Kenneth Adams
First Chef:	Arnold Yarrow
Fifth Waitress:	Ida Goldapple
Sixth Waitress:	Brenda Peters
Seventh Waitress:	Sandra Miller
Eighth Waitress:	Ann King
Mr Marango:	Nigel Davenport
Monique:	Anne Bishop
Head Waiter:	Cecil Brock
Tramp:	Patrick O'Connell
Director:	John Dexter

Serjeant Musgrave's Dance
by John Arden
22 October 1959
The Royal Court Theatre.

Private Sparky:	Donal Donnelly
Private Hurst:	Alan Dobie
Private Attercliffe:	Frank Finlay
Bludgeon, a bargee:	James Bree
Serjeant Musgrave:	Ian Bannen
The Parson:	Richard Caldicot
Mrs Hitchcock:	Freda Jackson
Annie:	Patsy Byrne
The Constable:	Michael Hunt
The Mayor:	Stratford Johns
A Slow Collier:	Jack Smethurst
A Pugnacious Collier:	Colin Blakely
Walsh, an earnest collier:	Harry Gwynn Davies
A Trooper of Dragoons:	Barry Wilsher
An Officer of Dragoons:	Clinton Greyn
Director:	Lindsay Anderson
Music:	Dudley Moore

Chicken Soup With Barley
by Arnold Wesker
7 June 1960
The Royal Court Theatre.

Sarah Kahn:	Kathleen Michael
Harry Kahn:	Frank Finlay
Monty Blatt:	Alan Howard
Dave Simmonds:	Mark Eden
Prince Silver:	Charles Kay
Hymie Kossof:	John Colin
Cissie Kahn:	Cherry Morris
Ada Kahn:	Ruth Meyers
Ronnie, as a boy:	Michael Phillips
Ronnie Kahn:	David Saire
Bessie Blatt:	Patsy Byrne
Director:	John Dexter

I'm Talking About Jerusalem
by Arnold Wesker
28 March 1960
The Belgrade Theatre, Coventry.

Ronnie Kahn:	George Tensotti
Ada Simmonds:	Cherry Morris
Sarah Kahn:	Lala Lloyd
Dave Simmonds:	Alan Howard
1st Removal Man:	Kenton Moore
2nd Removal Man:	Robin Parkinson
Libby Dobson:	Patrick O'Connell
Colonel Dewhurst:	Paul Kermack
Sammy:	Keith Crane
Danny Simmonds:	Peter Palmer
Esther Kahn:	Ann Robson
Cissie Kahn:	Rosemary Leach
Postman:	Rex Doyle
Director:	John Dexter

Trials by Logue
by Christopher Logue
23 November 1960
The Royal Court Theatre.

Antigone

Ismene:	Zoë Caldwell
Antigone:	Mary Ure
Head Steward:	Morris Perry
Second Steward:	Trevor Martin
Third Steward:	Murray Evans
Creon:	George Rose
Head Guard:	Dickie Owen
Second Guard:	Peter Fraser
Third Guard:	Tony Selby
Sentry:	Peter Duguid
Fourth Guard:	Laurence Harrington
Haemon:	Peter Holmes

Cob and Leach

Magistrate:	George Rose
Clerk of the Court:	Peter Duguid
First Policeman:	Morris Perry
Second Policeman:	Murray Evans
Whore:	Zoë Caldwell
Mabel Cob:	Mary Ure
Henry Leach:	Peter Fraser
Miss Edith Peaches:	Hazel Hughes
Sergeant Pokesdown:	Trevor Martin
Police Horse Charlotte:	Tony Selby & Dickie Owen
Plato (a dog):	Peter Holmes
Policewoman Suet (Bass):	Tony Stone
Constable Mogg (Drums):	Brian Pickles
Sergeant Posy (Piano):	Stanley Myers
Director:	Lindsay Anderson
Music:	Bill Le Sage

The Changeling
by Thomas Middleton & William Rowley
21 February 1961
The Royal Court Theatre.

Vermandero:	Peter Duguid
Tomazo de Piracquo:	David William
Alonzo de Piracquo:	Alan Howard
Alsemero:	Jeremy Brett
Jasperino:	Derek Newark
Alibius:	John Blatchley
Lollio:	Norman Rossington
Pedro:	Roland Curram
Antonio:	Robin Ray
Franciscus:	Charles Kay
De Flores:	Robert Shaw
Beatrice-Joanna:	Mary Ure
Diaphanta:	Annette Crosbie
Isabella:	Zoë Caldwell
Madmen, servants:	Pauline Munro Rita Tushingham Robin Chapman Derek Fuke Basil Moss Morris Perry
Director:	Tony Richardson
Costumes:	David Walker
Music:	Raymond Leppard
Dances:	Eleanor Fazan

Richard III
by William Shakespeare
24 May 1961
The Royal Shakespeare Theatre, Stratford-upon-Avon.

King Edward the Fourth:	Tony Church
Edward, Prince of Wales:	Michael Lewis
Richard, Duke of York:	Adrian Blount
George, Duke of Clarence:	Peter McEnery
Richard, Duke of Gloucester:	Christopher Plummer
Henry, Earl of Richmond:	Brian Murray
Cardinal Bourchier:	Julian Battersby
Archbishop of York:	Roger Jerome
Bishop of Ely:	Clifford Rose
Duke of Buckingham:	Eric Porter
Lord Hastings:	Colin Blakely
Lord Stanley:	Redmond Phillips
Earl Rivers:	Michael Murray
Marquis of Dorset:	Peter Holmes
Lord Grey:	Gareth Morgan
Duke of Norfolk:	Gordon Gostelow
Earl of Surrey:	Julian Battersby
Earl of Oxford:	David Buck
Sir James Blunt:	Russell Hunter
Lord Lovel:	Paul Bailey
Sir Richard Ratcliffe:	James Kerry
Sir William Catesby:	Ian Richardson
Sir James Tyrell:	David Buck
Sir Robert Brakenbury:	Clifford Rose
Tressel:	James Kerry
Berkeley:	Brian Wright
Lord Mayor of London:	William Wallis
A Pursuivant to Hastings:	Eric Flynn
A Priest:	Ronald Scott-Dodd
A Scrivener:	Terry Wale
Page:	Michael Warchus
First Murderer:	Gordon Gostelow
Second Murderer:	Russell Hunter
Margaret:	Edith Evans
Elizabeth:	Elizabeth Sellars
Duchess of York:	Esme Church
Lady Anne:	Jill Dixon
Daughter to Clarence:	Rosemary Mussell
Director:	Bill Gaskill
Designer's Assistant:	Sally Jacobs
Lighting:	Richard Pilbrow
Music:	Marc Wilkinson

Luther
by John Osborne
27 July 1961
The Royal Court Theatre, transferring to the Phoenix Theatre, 5 September 1961.

A Knight:	Julian Glover
The Prior at Erfurt:	James Cairncross
Martin Luther:	Albert Finney
Hans, his father:	Bill Owen
Lucas, a friend of Hans:	Peter Duguid
Brother Weinand:	Dan Meaden
John Tetzel:	Peter Bull
Johann von Staupitz:	George Devine
Cajetan, Cardinal of San Sisto:	John Moffatt
Karl von Miltitz:	Robert Robinson
Pope Leo the Tenth:	Charles Kay
John Eck:	James Cairncross
Katherine:	Meryl Gourley

Monks, Lords,
Peasants etc.: Stacey Davies
Murray Evans
Derek Fuke
Malcolm Taylor
Singers: John Kirk
Frank Davies
Andrew Pearmain
David Read
Children: Roger Harbird
Paul Large

Director: Tony Richardson
Music: John Addison
Chorus Master: John McCarthy

Tom Jones
a Woodfall film,
adapted from the novel by Henry
Fielding by John Osborne
1961

Tom Jones: Albert Finney
Sophie Western: Susannah York
Squire Western: Hugh Griffith
Miss Western: Edith Evans
Lady Bellaston: Joan Greenwood
Molly: Diane Cilento
Squire Allworthy: George Devine
Lord Fellamar: David Tomlinson
Mrs Miller: Rosalind Atkinson
Mrs Wilkins: Angela Baddeley
Thwackum: Peter Bull
Landlady: Avis Bunnage
Parson Supple: James Cairncross
Fitzpatrick: George A. Cooper
Northerton: Julian Glover
Mrs Seagrim: Freda Jackson
Bridget Allworthy: Rachel Kempson
Mrs Fitzpatrick: Rosalind Knight
Black George: Wilfred Lawson
Partridge: Jack MacGowran
Square: John Moffat
Dowling: Redmond Phillips
Mrs Waters: Joyce Redman
Honour: Patsy Rowlands
Blifil: David Warner

Produced and directed by Tony
Richardson

A Midsummer Night's Dream
by William Shakespeare
24 January 1962
The Royal Court Theatre.

Theseus: Robert Lang
Egeus: Morris Perry
Lysander: Corin Redgrave
Demetrius: Kenneth McReddie
Philostrate: Peter Froggatt
Quince: Ronnie Barker
Snug: Stuart Harris
Bottom: Colin Blakely
Flute: Nicol Williamson
Snout: David Warner
Starveling: James Bolam
Hippolyta: Yolande Bavan
Hermia: Rita Tushingham
Helena: Lynn Redgrave
Oberon: Colin Jeavons
Titania: Samantha Eggar
Puck: Alfred Lynch
First Fairy: Gillian Hoyle
Peaseblossom: Lesley Scoble
Cobweb: Teresa Scoble
Moth: Carol Dilworth
Mustardseed: Pauline Foreman

Director: Tony Richardson
Music: John Addison

Chips With Everything
by Arnold Wesker
27 April 1962
The Royal Court Theatre,
transferring to The Vaudeville
Theatre 13 June 1962.

Corporal Hill: Frank Finlay
239 Cannibal,
Archie: George Innes
252 Wingate
(Chas): Colin Campbell
276 Thompson
(Pip): John Kelland
247 Seaford
(Wilfe): Laurie Asprey
284 McClore,
Andrew: Alexander Balfour
272 Richardson
(Whitey): Colin Farrell
277 Cohen
(Dodger): Hugh Futcher
266 Smith
(Dickey): John Bull
279 Washington
(Smiler): Ronald Lacey
Wing
Commander: Martin Boddey
Squadron Leader: Robert Bruce
Pilot Officer: Corin Redgrave
P.T. Instructor: Michael Goldie
Recruit: Peter Kelly
Night Guard: Bruce Heighley
1st Corporal: Roger Heathcott
2nd Corporal: Michael Blackham
1st Airman: Michael Craze
2nd Airman: Alan Stevens

Director: John Dexter
Music: Colin Farrell
Drill instruction: ex RSM Brittain

Happy Days
by Samuel Beckett
1 November 1962
The Royal Court Theatre.

Winnie: Brenda Bruce
Willie: Peter Duguid

Director: George Devine

Baal
by Bertolt Brecht
(translated by Peter Tegel)
7 February 1963
Phoenix Theatre.

Ekart: Harry Andrews
Mech/Third
Woodman/
Gougon: James Mellor
Dr Poller/Priest/
First Man: Bernard Kay
Emile/Savettka: Vivian Pickles
Pschierer/Beggar: Harold Goodwin
First Young Man/
Pianist/First
Game Keeper: Henry Woolf
Young Woman/
Luise/Redhead: Guinevere Roberts
Second Young
Man/Lupu/First
Woodman: Terry Bale
Johannes: Tim Preece
Baal: Peter O'Toole
Waiter/Second Truck
Driver/First Farmer/
Second Man: Declan Mulholland
First Truck Driver/Fourth
Woodman/Second
Game Keeper: Morgan Sheppard
Third Truck Driver/
Second Farmer/
Bolleboll/Third
Man: Oliver MacGreevy
Johanna: Gemma Jones

Older Sister: Kate Binchy
Younger Sister: Annette Robertson
Landlady/Maja: Marie Kean
Sophie/Waitress: Mary Miller
Tramp/Landlord/
Watzmann: Arthur O'Sullivan
Mjurk/Second
Woodman/
Fourth Man: Trevor Martin

Director: Bill Gaskill

Skyvers
by Barry Reckord
23 July 1963
The Royal Court Theatre.

Cragge: David Hemmings
Brook: Philip Martin
Colman: Nicholas Edmett
Adams: John Hall
Jordan: Lance Kaufman
Freeman: Bernard Kay
Webster: John Woodvine
Headmaster: Dallas Cavell
Helen: Chloe Ashcroft
Sylvia: Annette Robertson

Director: Ann Jellicoe
Designer's
Assistant: Suzanne Glanister

Exit the King
by Eugene Ionesco
12 September 1963
The Royal Court Theatre.

The Guard: Peter Bayliss
King Berenger
the First: Alec Guinness
Queen
Marguerite: Googie Withers
Juliette: Eileen Atkins
Queen Marie: Natasha Parry
The Doctor: Graham Crowden

Director: George Devine

The Seagull
by Anton Chekhov
12 March 1964
The Queen's Theatre (The ESC).

Yakov: Malcolm Taylor
Workmen: Reginald Gillam &
Derek Fuke
Semyon
Semyonovich
Medvedenko: Philip Locke
Masha: Ann Beach
Pyotr
Nicolayevich
Sorin: Paul Rogers
Constantin
Gavrilovich
Treplev: Peter McEnery
Nina
Mikhailovna
Zerechnaya: Vanessa Redgrave
Polina
Andreyevna: Rachel Kempson
Yevgeny
Sergeyevich
Dorn: George Devine
Irina
Nikolayevna
Arkadina: Peggy Ashcroft
Boris
Aleksoyevich
Trigorin: Peter Finch
Ilya Afnasyevich
Shamrayev: Mark Dignam
Maid: Kate Binchy

Director: Tony Richardson
Music: John Addison

Play
by Samuel Beckett
7 April 1964
The Old Vic Theatre.

First Woman: Rosemary Harris
Second Woman: Billie Whitelaw
Man: Robert Stephens

Director: George Devine

Othello
by William Shakespeare
21 April 1964
The National Theatre at the Old Vic.

Roderigo: Michael Rothwell
Iago: Frank Finlay
Brabantio: Martin Boddey
Othello: Laurence Olivier
Cassio: Derek Jacobi
Senate Officers: Edward Petherbridge
& George Innes
Gratiano: Edward Caddick
Lodovico: Kenneth Mackintosh
Duke of Venice: Harry Lomax
Duke's Officer: Terence Knapp
Senator: Keith Marsh
Sailor: Tom Kempinski
Messenger: Peter John
Desdemona: Maggie Smith
Montano: Edward Hardwicke
Cypriot Officers: Roger Heathcott
Keith Marsh
Emilia: Joyce Redman
Herald: Neil Fitzpatrick
Bianca: Mary Miller

Director: John Dexter

Saint Joan of the Stockyards
by Bertolt Brecht
11 June 1964
The Queen's Theatre (The ESC).

J. Pierpoint
Mauler: Lionel Stander
Cridle: Dervis Ward
Joan Dark: Siobhan McKenna
Martha: Rachel Kempson
Jackson: Nicholas Smith
Graham: Mark Dignam
Lennox: Bruce Boa
Meyers: Denis Shaw
Sullivan Slift: Michael Medwin
Detective 1: Thick Wilson
Detective 2: Derek Fuke
Foreman: Roy Pattison
Young Lad: Dudley Hunte
Mrs
Luckerniddle: Patricia Connolly
Gloomb: Hal Galili
Other Man: Brian Anderson
Waiter: Clive Endersby
Paul Snyder: Robert Ayres
Mulberry: Malcolm Taylor
Worker's Leader: Bruce Boa
Second Leader: Roy Pattison
Reporter 1: Katie Fitzroy
Reporter 2: Desmond Stokes

Director: Tony Richardson
Music: John Addison

Inadmissible Evidence
by John Osborne
9 September 1964
The Royal Court Theatre,
transferred to The Wyndham's
Theatre, 17 May 1965.

Jones: John Quentin
Bill Maitland: Nicol Williamson
Hudson: Arthur Lowe

Shirley: Ann Beach
Joy: Lois Daine
Mrs Garnsey: Clare Kelly
Jane Maitland: Natasha Pyne
Liz: Sheila Allen

Director: Anthony Page
Assistant to the
director: Peter Gill
Assistant to the
designer: Brenda Briant
Sound: Marc Wilkinson

Julius Caesar
by William Shakespeare
26 November 1964
The Royal Court Theatre.

Flavius: Peter Brett
Marullus: Rex Robinson
Julius Caesar: Paul Curran
Casca: Graham Crowden
Calphurnia: Nan Munro
Mark Antony: Daniel Massey
A Soothsayer: Edwin Finn
Brutus: Ian Bannen
Cassius: T.P. McKenna
Cicero: Nicholas Grimshaw
Cinna: David Jackson
Decius Brutus: Robert McBain
Metellus Cimber: Anthony Hopkins
Trebonius: Lew Luton
Lucius: Malcolm Reynolds
Portia: Sheila Allen
Ligarius: Harry Hutchinson
Caesar's Servant: Douglas Ditta
Artemidorus: Milton Johns
Antony's
Servant: Stephen Moore
Octavius'
Captain: Rex Robinson
Cinna, the Poet: Milton Johns
Lepidus: Robert McBain
Octavius Caesar: Ronald Pickup
Strato: John Dunn Hill
Pindarus: Henry Stamper
Titinius: Stephen Moore
Messala: Peter Brett
A Poet: Harry Hutchinson

Director: Lindsay Anderson
Music: Marc Wilkinson

Mother Courage and her Children
by Bertolt Brecht
(translated by Eric Bentley
Lyrics translated by W.H. Auden)
12 May 1965
The National Theatre at the Old Vic.

Mother Courage: Madge Ryan
Kattrin: Lynn Redgrave
Eiliff: Mike Gambon
Swiss Cheese: George Innes
Recruiting Officer: Michael Turner
Sergeant: Colin Blakely
Cook: Frank Finlay
Swedish
Commander: Kenneth Mackintosh
Chaplain: Peter Collier
Ordnance Officer: Christopher Timothy
Yvette: Petronella Barker
Soldier with
Cannon: Nicholas Edmett
One-eye: Terence Knapp
Yvette's Colonel: Harry Lomax
Stretcher Bearers: Malcolm Terris &
Roy Holder
Catholic Sergeant: David Hargreaves
Clerk: Edward Hardwicke
Young Soldier: Tom Kempinski
Old Soldier: Keith Marsh

Soldier with Fur Coat:	Kenneth Mackintosh
Second Soldier:	Michael Turner
Peasant Woman:	Maggie Riley
Peasant:	Reginald Green
First Customer:	Terence Knapp
Second Customer:	Tom Kempinski
Young Man:	Nicholas Edmett
Old Woman:	Janie Booth
Yvette's Servant:	Roy Holder
Singer:	Sheila Reid
Lieutenant:	David Hargreaves
First Soldier:	Edward Hardwicke
Second Soldier:	Michael Turner
Third Soldier:	Malcolm Terris
Peasant Woman:	Barbara Hicks
Peasant:	Keith Marsh
Young Peasant:	Christopher Timothy
Director:	Bill Gaskill
Music:	Paul Dessau

A Patriot for Me
by John Osborne
30 June 1965
The Royal Court Theatre.

Alfred Redl:	Maximilian Schell
August Siczynski:	John Castle
Steinbauer:	Rio Fanning
Ludwig Max von Kupfer:	Frederick Jaeger
Kupfer's Seconds:	Lew Luton, Richard Morgan
Privates:	Tim Pearce, David Schurmann, Thick Wilson
Lt.-Col. Ludwig von Möhl:	Clive Morton
Adjutant:	Timothy Carlton
Maximilian von Taussig:	Edward Fox
Albrecht:	Sandor Eles
Waiters at Anna's:	Peter John, Domy Reiter
Officers:	Timothy Carlton, Lew Luton, Hal Hamilton, Richard Morgan
Whores:	Dona Martyn, Virginia Wetherell, Jackie Daryl, Sandra Hampton
Anna:	Laurel Mather
Hilde:	Jennifer Jayne
Stanitsin:	Desmond Perry
Col. Mischa Oblensky:	George Murcell
Gen. Conrad von Hotzendorf:	Sebastian Shaw
Countess Sophia Delyanoff:	Jill Bennett
Judge Advocate Jaroslav Kunz:	Ferdy Mayne
Flunkeys:	John Forbes, Richard Morgan, Peter John, Timothy Carlton
Hofburg Guests:	Cyril Wheeler, Douglas Sheldon, Bryn Bartlett, Dona Martyn, Virginia Wetherell, Jackie Daryl, Sandra Hampton, Laurel Mather
Café Waiters:	Anthony Roye, Domy Reiter, Bryn Bartlett, Cyril Wheeler
Group at table:	Dona Martyn, Lew Luton, Bryn Bartlett, Cyril Wheeler
Young Man in Café:	Paul Robert
Paul:	Douglas Sheldon
Privates:	Richard Morgan, David Schurmann, Tim Pearce, Thick Wilson
Baron von Epp:	George Devine
Ferdy:	John Forbes
Figaro:	Thick Wilson
Lt. Stefan Kovacs:	Hal Hamilton
Marie-Antoinette:	Lew Luton
Tsarina:	Domy Reiter
Lady Godiva:	Peter John
Ball Guests:	Cyril Wheeler, Richard Morgan, Timothy Carlton, John Castle, Edward Fox, Paul Robert
Flunkey:	David Schurmann
Shepherdesses:	Franco Derosa, Robert Kidd
Dr Schoepfer:	Vernon Dobtcheff
Boy:	Franco Derosa
2nd Lt. Victor Jerzabek:	Tim Pearce
Hotel Waiters:	Bryn Bartlett, Lew Luton
Orderly:	Richard Morgan
Mischa Lipschutz:	David Schurmann
Mitzi Heigel:	Virginia Wetherell
Minister:	Anthony Roye
Voices of Deputies:	Clive Morton, Sebastian Shaw, George Devine, Vernon Dobtcheff, Cyril Wheeler
Director:	Anthony Page
Musical Director:	Tibor Kunstler

The Lion and the Jewel
by Wole Soyinka
12 December 1966
The Royal Court Theatre.

Sidi:	Hannah Bright-Taylor
Lakunlo:	Femi Euba
Baroka:	Lionel Ngakane
Sadiku:	Jumoko Debayo
The Favourite:	Trudi Coleman
The Wrestler:	Ilarrio Pedro
Director:	Desmond O'Donovan
Music:	Marc Wilkinson & Sanya Dousanmu

Ghosts
by Ibsen
(translation by Denis Cannon)
14 June 1967
RSC at The Aldwych.

Regina:	Chloe Ashcroft
Engstrand:	Clifford Rose
Pastor Manders:	David Waller
Mrs Alving:	Peggy Ashcroft
Oswald:	John Castle
Director:	Alan Bridges
Lighting:	David Read

Orpheus and Euridice
by Gluck
4 October 1967
Sadler's Wells Theatre.

Orpheus:	Alexander Young
Cupid:	Margaret Neville
A Blessed Spirit:	Margaret Curphey
Euridice:	Patricia Kern
Producer:	Glen Byam Shaw
Conductor:	Bryan Balkwill
Choreographer:	Peter Darrell
Lighting:	Charles Bristow

Isadora
(film) based on 'My Life'
by Isadora Duncan *and*
'Isadora Duncan, An Intimate Portrait' by Sewell Stokes,
screenplay by Melvyn Bragg & Clive Exton, with additional dialogue by Margaret Drabble
Universal City Studios
1968

Isadora:	Vanessa Redgrave
Gordon Craig:	James Fox
Paris Singer:	Jason Robards
Sergei Essenin:	Ivan Tchenko
Roger:	John Fraser
Mrs Duncan:	Bessie Love
Mary Desti:	Cynthia Harris
Elizabeth Duncan:	Libby Glenn
Raymond Duncan:	Tony Vogel
Archer:	Wallas Eaton
Pim:	John Quentin
Bedford:	Nicholas Pennell
Miss Chase:	Ronnie Gilbert
Armand:	Christian Duvalex
Raucous Woman:	Margaret Courtenay
Hearty Husaband:	Arthur White
Alicia:	Iza Teller
Bugatti:	Vladimir Leskovar
Mr Stirling:	John Warner
Russian Teacher:	Ina De La Haye
Gospel Billy:	John Brandon
Deirdre:	Lucinda Chambers
Patrick:	Simon Lutton
Davies Isadora's Tour Manager:	Alan Gifford
Producers:	Robert & Raymond Hakim
Director:	Karel Reisz
Lighting Cameraman:	Larry Pizer
Camera Operator:	Dennis Lewiston
Art Directors:	Michael Seymour & Ralph Brinton
Music:	Maurice Jarre
Choreographer:	Litz Pisk

If...
screenplay by David Sherwin & Lindsay Anderson (Paramount)
A Memorial Enterprises Film
1968

Mick:	Malcolm McDowell
Johnny:	David Wood
Wallace:	Richard Warwick
Rowntree:	Robert Swann
The Girl:	Christine Noonan
Denson:	Hugh Thomas
Bobby Philips:	Rupert Webster
Headmaster:	Peter Jeffrey
General Denson:	Anthony Nicholls
Mr Kemp:	Arthur Lowe
Matron:	Mona Washbourne
Mrs Kemp:	Mary MacLeod
Chaplain:	Geoffrey Chater
John Thomas:	Ben Aris
Stephans:	Guy Ross
Biles:	Brian Pettifer
Jute:	Sean Bury
Fortinbras:	Michael Cadman
Barnes:	Peter Sproule
Keating:	Robin Askwith
History Master:	Graham Crowden
Classics Master:	Charles Lloyd Pack
Pussy Graves:	Richard Everett
Peanuts:	Philip Bagenal
Cox:	Nicholas Page
Fisher:	Robert Yetzes
Willens:	David Griffin
Van Eyssen:	Graham Sharman
Baird:	Richard Tombleson
Machin:	Richard Davies
Brunning:	Michael Newport
Markland:	Charles Sturridge
Hunter:	Martin Beaumont
Music Master:	John Garrie
School Porter:	Tommy Godfrey
Producers:	Michael Medwin & Lindsay Anderson
Director:	Lindsay Anderson
Assistant director:	John Stoneman
Director of photography:	Miroslav Ondricek
Cameraman:	Charles Menges
Costumes:	Shura Cohen
Music:	Marc Wilkinson

Life Price
by Michael O'Neill & Jeremy Seabrook
13 January 1969
The Royal Court Theatre.

Women:	June Brown, Christine Hargreaves, Mary Macleod, Tina Packer, June Watson
Rube:	Diana Coupland
Den:	Derek Carpenter
Ray:	Anthony Sagar
Vi:	Thelma Whiteley
Chief Inspector:	Alec Ross
Policemen:	Philip Woods, Edward Clayton
Reporter:	Philip Woods
Manager of a Credit House:	James Mellor
Secretary:	Yvonne Antrobus
May:	Mary Macleod
Stan:	Anthony Douse
Teresa:	Julie Kennard
Female Social Worker:	Yvonne Antrobus
Television Director:	Allan Mitchell
Female Television Personality:	Yvonne Antrobus
Psychiatrist:	Allan Mitchell
Churchman:	Patrick Godfrey
Director:	Peter Gill
Designer's Assistant:	Andrew Sanders

Hamlet
by William Shakespeare
18 February 1969
The Roundhouse (also filmed).

Hamlet:	Nicol Williamson
Claudius:	Anthony Hopkins
Gertrude:	Judy Parfitt
Polonius:	Mark Dignam
Ophelia:	Marianne Faithful
Laertes:	Michael Pennington
Horatio:	Gordon Jackson
Francisco:	Robin Chadwick
Barnardo:	John Trenaman
Marcellus:	John J. Carney
Reynaldo:	Roger Lloyd Pack
Rosencrantz:	Ben Aris
Guildenstern:	Clive Graham
First Player:	Roger Livesey
Player Queen:	Richard Everett
Player King:	John J. Carney
A captain:	John Railton
Messenger:	Mark Griffith
First sailor:	Michael Elphick
Gravedigger:	Roger Livesey
A priest:	Ian Collier
Osric:	Peter Gale
Courtiers, Soldiers, Players:	Robin Chadwick, Ian Collier, Michael Elphick, Richard Everett, Mark Griffith, Anjelica Huston, Bill Jarvis, Roger Lloyd Pack, John Railton, John Trenaman, Jennifer Tudor
Director:	Tony Richardson
Music:	Patrick Gowers

Three Months Gone
by Donald Howarth
28 January 1970
The Royal Court Theatre, transferred to The Duchess Theatre 4 March 1970.

Anna Bowers:	Jill Bennett
Maurice Bowers:	Alan Lake
Alvin Hanker:	Richard O'Callaghan
Mrs Hanker:	Diana Dors
Doctor Franklyn:	Kevin Stoney
A Milkman:	Warren Clarke
Director:	Ronald Eyre

Beckett/3
31 March 1970
Theatre Upstairs, The Royal Court Theatre.

Come and Go
Flo:	Gillian Martell
Vi:	Queenie Watts
Ru:	Susan Williamson
Director:	Bill Gaskill

Cascando
Opener:	Kenneth Cranham
Voice:	Stanley Lebor
Director:	Roger Croucher

Play
M:	Kenneth Cranham
W1:	Gillian Martell
W2:	Susan Williamson
Director:	Bill Gaskill

Home
by David Storey
17 June 1970
The Royal Court Theatre.

Harry:	John Gielgud
Jack:	Ralph Richardson
Marjorie:	Dandy Nichols
Kathleen:	Mona Washbourne
Alfred:	Warren Clarke
Director:	Lindsay Anderson
Lighting:	Andy Phillips
Music:	Alan Price

Ned Kelly
(film)
1970

Cast included:
Ned Kelly:	Mick Jagger
Dan Kelly:	Alan Bickford
Steve Hart:	Geoff Gilmour
Jo Byrne:	Mark McManus
Wild Wright:	Serge Lazaress
Director:	Tony Richardson

A Woman Killed With Kindness
by Thomas Heywood
7 April 1971
The National Theatre at the Old Vic.

Jenkin:	Dai Bradley
Sisly Milkpail:	Jo Maxwell-Miller
Sir Francis Acton:	Tom Baker
Wendoll:	Frank Barrie
Master John Frankford:	Anthony Hopkins
Sir Charles Mountford:	Derek Jacobi
Master Cranwell:	Michael Tudor Barnes
Master Malby:	Tom Georgeson
Mistress Anne Frankford:	Joan Plowright
Nicholas:	Paul Curran
Jack Slime:	Alan Duley
Roger Brickbat:	Brian Jameson
Susan Mountford:	Louise Purnell
Sheriff:	Peter Rocca
Spiggot:	Benjamin Whitrow
A Keeper:	Michael Edgar
Old Mountford:	Alan Dudley
Master Shafton:	Barry James
Master Sandy:	Michael Edgar
Master Rodon:	Tom Dickinson
Master Tydy:	David Howey
A Jailer:	Peter Rocca
Servant:	Howard Southern
Director:	John Dexter

Tyger
by Adrian Mitchell
20 July 1971
The National Theatre at The New.

William Blake:	Gerald James
Kate Blake:	Jane Wenham
Sir Joshua Rat:	John Moffatt
Scofield:	Denis Quilley
Home Secretary:	Anthony Nicolls
Rev. Trussler/ William Shakespeare:	Michael Turner
Walt Whitman/ Working Man:	Bernard Gallagher
King George:	Bill Fraser
Lady Twat:	Hazel Hughes
Isabelle:	Isabelle Lucas
Klopstock/ John Milton:	David Ryall
1st Intellectual/ Robert Browning:	David Kincaid
2nd Intellectual/ Rudyard Kipling:	Tony Leary
3rd Intellectual/ Robert Southey/ Edward Lear:	James Hayes
Barmaid:	Maggie Riley
Civil Servant/ Evelyn Graze:	Malcolm Reid
The Crab/Allen Ginsberg:	Ian Burford
Ghost of a Flea:	Peter Smart
Postman:	Anthony Barnett
Randy Women:	Sarah Atkinson Maureen Lipman Louise Ramsay
Lord Nobodaddy/ Geoffrey Chaucer:	David Henry
Mechanical Creature/ John Keats:	Peter Duncan
Henry Fuseli:	Ray Callaghan
Samuel Palmer:	John Gulliver
William Wordsworth:	Alan Jackson
Percy Bysshe Shelley:	Dave Wintour
Samuel Coleridge:	Riggs O'Hara

Lord Byron:	Norman Beaton
Working Man's Wife:	Mary Griffiths
His Family:	Jean Boht Anthony Barnett Peter Duncan
Captain Stedman/ Alfred Tennyson:	Denis Lill
Directors:	Michael Blakemore & John Dexter

Designed with William Dudley

The Changing Room
by David Storey
9 November 1971
The Royal Court Theatre,
transferred to The Globe Theatre
15 December 1971.

Harry:	John Barrett
Patsy:	Jim Norton
Fielding:	David Daker
Mic Morley:	Edward Peel
Kendal:	Warren Clarke
Luke:	Don McKillop
Fenchurch:	Peter Childs
Colin Jagger:	Mark McManus
Trevor:	Michael Elphick
Walsh:	Edward Judd
Sandford:	Brian Glover
Barry Copley:	Geoffrey Hinsliff
Jack Stringer:	David Hill
Bryan Atkinson:	Peter Schofield
Billy Spencer:	Alun Armstrong
John Clegg:	Matthew Guinness
Frank Moore:	John Price
Danny Crosby:	Barry Keegan
Cliff Owens:	Frank Mills
Tallon:	Brian Lawson
Thornton:	Paul Dawkins
Mackendrick:	John Rae
Director:	Lindsay Anderson
Lighting:	Andy Phillips
Assistant designer:	Jenny Holland

Krapp's Last Tape
by Samuel Beckett
16 January 1973
The Royal Court Theatre.

Krapp:	Albert Finney
Director:	Anthony Page
Lighting:	Rory Dempster

Not I
by Samuel Beckett
16 January 1973
The Royal Court Theatre.

Mouth:	Billie Whitelaw
Auditor:	Brian Miller
Director:	Anthony Page
Lighting:	Rory Dempster

Savages
by Christopher Hampton
12 April 1973
The Royal Court Theatre,
transferred to the Comedy Theatre
20 June 1973.

Alan West:	Paul Scofield
Mrs West:	Rona Anderson
Carlos:	Tom Conti
Crawshaw:	Michael Pennington
General:	Leonard Kavanagh
Attorney-General/ Investigator:	Gordon Sterne
Ataide Pereira:	Glyn Grain

Major Brigg:	A.J. Brown
Chief/Bert:	Frank Singuineau
Elmer Penn:	Geoffrey Palmer
Kumai:	Terence Burns
Pilot:	Leonard Kavanagh
Indians:	George Baizley Lynda Dagley Thelma Kidger Donna Louise Eddy Nedari J.C. Shepherd
Director:	Robert Kidd
Assistant Director:	Robert Fox
Lighting:	Andy Phillips

Designed with Andrew Sanders

Cromwell
by David Storey
15 August 1973
The Royal Court Theatre.

Logan:	Jarlath Conroy
O'Halloran:	Albert Finney
Morgan:	Alun Armstrong
Proctor:	Brian Cox
Chamberlain:	Colin Douglas
Moore:	John Barrett
Matthew:	Mark McManus
Margaret:	Anne Dyson
Joan:	Frances Tomelty
Kennedy:	Martin Read
Broome:	Peter Postlethwaite
Cleet:	Kenneth Colley
Wallace:	Alun Armstrong
Drake:	Colin Bennett
Boatman:	Colin Douglass
Soldiers:	Conrad Asquith Forbes Collins Alan Ford Mike Melia
Travellers:	John Barrett Anne Dyson Alan Ford Mike Melia Diana Rayworth
Director:	Anthony Page
Assistant Director:	Anton Gill
Lighting:	Andy Phillips

O Lucky Man!
(film)
1973

Mick Travis:	Malcolm McDowell
Monty/Sir James Burgess:	Ralph Richardson
Gloria/Mint Paillard/ Mrs Richards:	Rachael Roberts
Mr Duff/Charlie Johnson/Dr Mu:	Arthur Lowe
Patricia:	Helen Mirren
Sister Hallett/Usher/ Neighbour:	Mona Washbourne
Director:	Lindsay Anderson

Life Class
by David Storey
9 April 1974
The Royal Court Theatre.

Allott:	Alan Bates
Warren:	Stephen Bent
Saunders:	Frank Grimes
Stella:	Rosemary Martin
Mathews:	Paul Kelly
Brenda:	Sally Watts
Carter:	David Lincoln
Catherine:	Gabrielle Lloyd
Mooney:	Stuart Rayner

Gillian:	Brenda Cavendish
Abercrombie:	Bob Peck
Foley:	Brian Glover
Philips:	Gerald James
Director:	Lindsay Anderson
Assistant Director:	Anton Gill
Lighting:	Nick Chelton

Pygmalion
by George Bernard Shaw
16 May 1974
The Albery Theatre.

Clara Eynsford Hill:	Sarah Atkinson
Mrs Eynsford Hill:	Margaret Ward
A Bystander:	Dennis Handby
Freddy Eynsford Hill:	Anthony Naylor
Eliza Doolittle:	Diana Rigg
Colonel Pickering:	Jack May
Professor Higgins:	Alec McCowen
Sarcastic Bystander:	Simon MacCorkindale
Bystanders & crowd:	Fred Bryant John Church Joyce Donaldson Jack Eden Tony Leary Angela Wallbank Jeremy Wallis
Mrs Pearce:	Hilda Fenemore
Alfred Doolittle:	Bob Hoskins
Mrs Higgins:	Ellen Pollock
Palour Maid:	Melanie Peck
Director:	John Dexter
Lighting:	Andy Philllips

Designed with Andrew Sanders

What The Butler Saw
by Joe Orton
16 July 1975
The Royal Court Theatre.

Dr Prentice:	Michael Medwin
Geraldine Barclay:	Jane Carr
Mrs Prentice:	Betty Marsden
Nicholas Beckett:	Kevin Lloyd
Dr Rance:	Valentine Dyall
Sergeant Match:	Brian Glover
Director:	Lindsay Anderson
Lighting:	Nick Chelton
Music:	Alan Price

Teeth 'n' Smiles
by David Hare
2 September 1975
The Royal Court Theatre.

Arthur/ Songwriter:	Jack Shepherd
Inch/Roadie:	Karl Howman
Laura/P.R.:	Cherie Lunghi
Nash/Drummer:	Rene Augustus
Wilson/Keyboard:	Mick Ford
Snead/Porter:	Roger Hume
Peyote/ Bass Guitar:	Hugh Fraser
Smegs/ Lead Guitar:	Andrew Dickson
Anson/Student:	Antony Sher
Maggie/Vocals:	Helen Mirren
Saraffian/ Manager:	Dave King
Randolph/Star:	Heinz with Ian Elliott & David Charkham
Director:	David Hare
Lighting:	Jack Raby
Music:	Nick Bicât

That Time
by Samuel Beckett
20 May 1976
The Royal Court Theatre.

Listener:	Patrick Magee
Director:	Donald McWhinnie

Footfalls
by Samuel Beckett
20 May 1976
The Royal Court Theatre.

M:	Billie Whitelaw
V:	Rose Hill
Director:	Samuel Beckett

Rum an' Coca-Cola
by Mustapha Matura
3 November 1976
The Royal Court Theatre.

Creator:	Norman Beaton
Bird:	Trevor Thomas
Director:	Donald Howarth

The Merchant
by Arnold Wesker
16 November 1977
The Plymouth Theatre, New York.

Shylock Kolner:	Joseph Leon
Jessica:	Julie Garfield
Rivka:	Marian Seldes
Tubal di Ponti:	John Seitz
Antonio Querini:	John Clements
Bassanio Visconti:	Nicolas Surovy
Lorenzo Pisani:	Everett McGill
Graziano Sanudo:	Riggs O'Hara
Portia Contarini:	Roberta Maxwell
Nerissa:	Gloria Gifford
Solomon Usque:	Jeffrey Horowitz
Rebecca de Mendes:	Angela Wood
Moses of Castelazzo:	Leib Lensky
Girolamo Priuli:	William Roerick
Abtalion da Modena:	Boris Tumarin
Maid/Singer:	Rebecca Malka
Servants/Senators:	Russ Banham Mark Blum Philip Carroll James David Cromar Brian Meister John Tyrrell

(Joseph Leon took over the role of Shylock after Zero Mostel's death just as the play opened.)

Director:	John Dexter
Lighting:	Andy Phillips

La Forza del Destino
by Giuseppe Verdi
2 February 1977
Théâtre National de l'Opéra, Paris.

Il Marchese de Calatrava:	Jules Bastin
Donna Leonora:	Martina Arroyo
Don Carlo di Vargas:	Norman Mittelmann
Don Alvaro:	Placido Domingo
Preziosilla:	Fiorenza Cossotto
Padre Guardiano:	Martti Talvela
Fra Melitone:	Gabriel Bacquier
Mastro Trabuco:	Michel Senechal
Director:	John Dexter
Conductor:	Julius Rudel
Lighting:	Andy Phillips

Designed with Andrew Sanders

Lulu
by Alban Berg
18 March 1977
Metropolitan Opera, New York.

Lulu:	Carole Farley
Dr. Schön:	Donald Gramm
Jack the Ripper:	Donald Gramm
Alwa:	Willian Lewis
Countess Geschwitz:	Tatiana Troyanos
Schigolch:	Andrew Foldi
The Ringmaster:	Lenus Carlson
The Acrobat:	Lenus Carlson
The Physician:	Peter Sliker
The Painter:	Raymond Gibbs
The Prince:	Nico Castel
The Manservant:	Nico Castel
The Marquis:	Nico Castel
Wardrobe Mistress:	Cynthia Munzer
The Schoolboy:	Cynthia Munzer
The Stage Manager:	Richard Best
Director:	John Dexter
Conductor:	James Levine
Lighting:	Gil Wechsler

Saratoga
by Bronson Howard
13 December 1978
The RSC at the Aldwych.

Robert Sackett:	Dennis Waterman
Jack Benedict:	James Laurenson
Papa Vanderpool:	Brian Hayes
The Hon. William Carter:	Jeffery Dench
Remington Pere:	James Berwick
Sir Mortimer Mutton-Legge:	Alan David
Mr Cornelius Wethertree:	Paul Imbusch
Major Luddington Whist:	Michael Bertenshaw
Frederick Augustus Carter:	Billie Brown
Frank Littlefield:	Stephen Jenn
Gyp:	Keith Hodiak
Reg:	Reginald Tsiboe
Sam:	Kelvin Omard
The Artist:	David Shaw-Parker
Effie Remington:	Polly James
Lucy Carter:	Cherie Lunghi
Olivia Alston:	Sheila Reid
Virginia Vanderpool:	Joanna McCallum
Mrs Vanderpool:	Maxine Audley
Lilly Livingston:	Denyse Alexander
Guests:	Shirley King
	Roger Martin
	Deirdra Morris
	Peter Tullo
Director:	Ronald Eyre
Assistant Director:	Mark Dornford-May
Music:	Carl Davis
Lights:	Brian Harris

Happy Days
by Samuel Beckett
7 June 1979
The Royal Court Theatre.

Winnie:	Billie Whitelaw
Willie:	Leonard Fenton
Director:	Samuel Beckett
Lighting:	Jack Raby

Die Entführung aus dem Serail
by Wolfgang Amadeus Mozart
12 October 1979
Metropolitan Opera, New York.

Belmonte:	Nicolai Gedda
Osmin:	Kurt Moll
Pedrillo:	Norbert Orth
Pasha Selim:	Werner Klemperer
Konstanze:	Edda Moser
Blondchen:	Norma Burrowes
Director:	John Dexter
Conductor:	James Levine
Lighting:	Gil Wechsler

The Rise and Fall of the City of Mahagonny
by Bertolt Brecht
16 November 1979
Metropolitan Opera, New York.

Fatty:	Ragnar Ulfung
Trinity Moses:	Cornell MacNeil
Leocadia Begbick:	Astrid Varnay
Jenny:	Teresa Stratas
Six Girls of Mahagonny:	Klara Barlow
	Nedda Casei
	Gwynn Cornell
	Joann Grillo
	Isola Jones
	Louise Wohlafka
Jimmy Mahoney:	Richard Cassilly
Jacob Schmidt:	Arturo Sergi
Moneybags Billy:	Vern Shinall
Alaska Wolf Joe:	Paul Plishka
Announcer:	Nico Castel
Toby Higgins:	Michael Best
Director:	John Dexter
Conductor:	James Levine
Lighting:	Gil Wechsler

Early Days
by David Storey
31 March 1980
Brighton Theatre Royal, opening at The National Theatre in The Cottesloe 22 April 1980.

Kitchen:	Ralph Richardson
Bristol:	Norman Jones
Mathilda:	Rosemary Martin
Benson:	Gerald Flood
Doctor:	Michael Bangerter
Gloria:	Barbara Flynn
Stephen:	Peter Machin
Director:	Lindsay Anderson
Assistant to the designer:	Carmel Collins
Lighting:	Nick Chelton
Music:	Alan Price

The Life of Galileo
by Bertolt Brecht
(translated by Howard Brenton)
13 August 1980
The Olivier Theatre.

The Speaker:	Robert Oates
Galileo Galilei:	Michael Gambon
Andrea Sarti:	Marc Brenner (Andrea as a boy)
Signora Sarti:	Yvonne Bryceland
Ludovico Marsili:	Elliott Cooper
Signor Priuli:	Andrew Cruickshank
Sagredo:	Nicholas Selby
The Doge of Venice:	Norman Rutherford
Senator:	Nigel Bellairs
Virginia:	Selina Cadell
Cosimo de'Medici:	Timothy Norton (as a boy)

Court Chamberlain:	Edmond Bennett
Theologian:	Gordon Whiting
Philosopher:	Daniel Thorndike
Mathematician:	Michael Beint
Federzoni:	James Hayes
Lady in Waiting:	Peggy Marshall
Younger Lady in Waiting:	Jill Stanford
Fat Prelate:	Artro Morris
First Astronomer:	Roger Gartland
Second Astronomer:	Peter Needham
Philosopher:	Robert Howard
Monk:	Nigel Bellairs
Thin Monk:	Adam Norton
Scholar:	Glenn Williams
Very old Cardinal:	Harry Lomax
The Cardinal's Monk:	Robert Ralph
Father Christopher Clavius:	Brian Kent
Fulganzio, the little Monk:	Simon Callow
Door Keeper:	Peter Harding
First secretary:	Peter Dawson
Second secretary:	Melvyn Bedford
Cardinal Barberini:	Basil Henson
Cardinal Bellarmin:	Mark Dignam
The Cardinal Inquisitor:	Stephen Moore
Andrea Sarti:	Michael Thomas (as a young man)
Filippo Mucius:	Michael Beint
The Ballad Singer:	Peter Land
The Ballad Singer's Wife:	Sandra Fehr
An Individual:	William Sleigh
Signor Vanni:	Kenneth Mackintosh
Signor Mincio:	Peter Needham
Cosimo de'Medici:	Roger Gartland
High Official:	Robert Howard
Monk on Guard:	Nigel Bellairs
Frontier Guard:	Glenn Williams
First Boy:	Adam Stafford
Second Boy:	Marc Brenner
Third Boy:	David Stone
Clerk:	Gordon Whiting
Director:	John Dexter
Designer's Assistant:	Peter Hartwell
Lighting:	Andy Phillips
Music Director:	Dominic Muldowney

Hamlet
by William Shakespeare
15 May 1981
Theatre Royal, Stratford East.

Claudius:	Del Henney
Hamlet:	Frank Grimes
Polonius:	Bob Hornery
Horatio:	Peter Holmes
Laertes:	Tim Woodward
Gertrude:	Colette O'Neil
Ophelia:	Cora Kinnaird
Voltemand:	Paul Geoffrey
Cornelius:	Edward Hibbert
Rosencrantz:	Mike Grady
Guildenstern:	Edward Arthur
Francisco:	Alan Penn
Marcellus:	Paul McCleary
Bernardo:	Robert Pugh
Ghost:	Trevor Martin
Player Queen:	Robin Langford
Gravedigger:	Bob Todd
Guard:	Robert Packham
Director:	Lindsay Anderson
Lighting:	Alan Jacobi

The Oresteia
by Aeschylus
(in a version by Tony Harrison)
28 November 1981
The National Theatre in the Olivier.

The parts were divided amongst the company:

Sean Baker, David Bamber, James Carter, Timothy Davies, Peter Dawson, Philip Donaghy, Roger Gartland, James Hayes, Greg Hicks, Kenny Ireland, Alfred Lynch, John Normington, Tony Robinson, David Roper, Barrie Rutter, Michael Thomas

Director:	Peter Hall
Music:	Harrison Birtwistle
Lighting:	John Bury
Assistant Designer:	Sue Jenkinson
Assistant Designer (Masks):	Jenny West

The Portage to San Cristobal of A.H.
by George Steiner, adapted for the stage by Christopher Hampton
17 February 1982
The Mermaid Theatre.

Simeon:	Morgan Sheppard
Gideon Benasseraf:	Bernard Kay
John Asher:	David Sumner
Elie Barach:	Harry Landis
Isaac Amsel:	John Salthouse
Emmanuel Lieber:	Sebastian Shaw
Guard:	Brian Attree
Old Man:	Francisco Morales
A.H.:	Alec McCowen
Professor Sir Evelyn Ryder:	Benjamin Whitrow
Bennett:	John Savident
Hoving:	Graham Callan
Colonel Shepilov:	John Savident
Nikolai Maximovitch Gruzdev:	Benjamin Whitrow
Rodriguez Kulken:	Barry Stanton
Indian Woman:	Stella Maris
Marvin Crownbacker:	Norman Chancer
Teku:	Jeffrey Vanderbyl
Dr Gervinus Röthling:	Benjamin Whitrow
Anna Elisabeth Röthling:	Laura Davenport
Rolf Hanfmann:	Graham Callan
Indian:	Francisco Morales
Blaise Josquin:	John Savident
V:	Laura Davenport
Avery Lockyer:	Benjamin Whitrow
Director:	John Dexter
Lighting:	Andy Phillips

Heartbreak House
by George Bernard Shaw
10 March 1983
Haymarket Theatre.

Ellie Dunn:	Mel Martin
Nurse Guinness:	Doris Hare
Captain Shotover:	Rex Harrison
Ariadne Utterword:	Rosemary Harris
Hesione Hushabye:	Diana Rigg
Mazzine Dunn:	Paul Curran
Hector Hushabye:	Paxton Whitehead
Boss Mangan:	Frank Middlemass
Randall Utterword:	Simon Ward
Billy Dunn:	Charles Rea
Director:	John Dexter
Lighting:	Andy Phillips

Hotel New Hampshire
(film)
1983

Cast included:

John Berry:	Rob Lowe
Franny Berry:	Jodie Foster
Frank Berry:	Paul McCrane
Win Berry:	Beau Bridges
Mary Berry:	Lisa Baines
Lily Berry:	Jennie Dundas
Egg Berry:	Seth Greene
Director:	Tony Richardson

The Devil and the Good Lord
by Jean-Paul Sartre
translated by Frank Hauser
6 September 1984
The Lyric Theatre, Hammersmith.

Prophet:	Carl Chase
Bishop:	Arthur Cox
Schmidt:	Mark Sproston
Hasty:	Stephen Boxer
Archbishop:	John Moreno
Archbishop's servant:	James Leslau
Lineheart:	David Ericsson
Heinz:	Michael Packer
Mother:	Julia McCarthy
Heinrich:	Simon Ward
Karl:	Sean Baker
Herman:	Daniel Davies
Goetz:	Gerard Murphy
Franz:	Brian Attree
Catherine:	Veronica Duffy
Banker:	John Moreno
Schulheim:	Carl Chase
Nossak:	David Ericsson
Reischel:	John Moreno
Little monk:	James Leslau
Little monk:	Delaval Astley
Tetzel:	Arthur Cox
Leper:	John Moreno
Hilda:	Maia Simon
Instructress:	Sally Thompson
Peasant:	David Chandler
Witch:	Sally Dexter
Drummer Boy:	Simon Elliot
Director:	John Dexter
Director's Assistant:	Simon van der Borgh
Lighting:	Andy Phillips

Gigi
by Lerner & Loewe,
based on a story by Colette
17 September 1985
The Lyric Theatre, Shaftesbury Avenue.

Honoré Lachailles:	Jean-Pierre Aumont
Gaston Lachailles:	Geoffrey Burridge
Liane d'Exelmans:	Carrie Ellis
Waiters:	Piers Henschel & Simon Elliott
Inez Alvarez (Mamita):	Beryl Reid
Gigi:	Amanda Waring
Alicia's Footmen:	Julian Ochyra & Dursley McLinden
Aunt Alicia:	Sian Phillips
Charles/Head Waiter:	Rex Robinson
Maneul/Maitre de Fresne/ Telephone Installer:	John Aron
Page Boy:	Lorraine Croft

Madame Leverne: Paula Jensen
Maitre Duclos/
Hotel Manager: David de Van
Lucille: Alexandra Denman
Ensemble: Mary-Louise Clark
Alexandra Denman
Loraine Croft
Tracey Wilson
Paula Jensen
Simon Elliott
Piers Henschel
David de Van
Dursley McLinden
Julian Ochyra

Director: John Dexter
Musical Director: Ray Cook
Lighting: Andy Phillips

The Mask of Orpheus
by Harrison Birtwistle
21 May 1986
English National Opera at the
London Coliseum.

Orpheus:
The Man: Philip Langridge
The Hero: Graham Walters
The Myth/
Hades: Nigel Robson

Euridice:
The Woman: Jean Rigby
The Hero: Zena Dilke
The Myth/Persephone:
Ethna Robinson

Aristaeus:
The Man: Tom McDonnell
The Hero: Robert Williams
The Myth/
Charon: Rodney Macann

The Oracle of the Dead/Hecate:
Marie Angel

The Troupe of Ceremony/Judges of the Dead
The Caller: Richard Angas
First Priest: Mark Curtis
Second Priest: John Kitchiner
Third Priest: Richard Suart

The Three Women/Furies
First Woman: Janis Kelly
Second Woman: Kate McCarney
Third Woman: Tamsin Dives

The Troupe of Passing Clouds:
Ian Cameron
Michael Knapp
Peter Neathey
Marcus Pearman
Linda Coggin
Mollie Guilfoyle
Kirsten Soar

Conductor: Elgar Howarth
Producer: David Freeman
Lighting: Andy Phillips

The Whales of August
screenplay by David Berry
An Alive Films Production with
Circle Associates Ltd.
1987

Sarah Webber: Lilian Gish
Libby Strong: Bette Davis
Mr Maranov: Vincent Price
Tisha Doughty: Ann Sothern
Joshua Brackett: Harry Carey Jr.
Mr Beckwith: Frank Grimes
Old Randall: Frank Pitkin
Young Randall: Mike Bush
Young Libby: Margaret Ladd
Young Tisha: Tisha Sterling
Young Sarah: Mary Steenburgen

Director: Lindsay Anderson
Director of
Photography: Mike Flash
Producers: Carolyn Peeiffer &
Mike Kaplan
Music: Alan Price

J.J. Farr
by Ronald Harwood
18 November 1987
Phoenix Theatre.

Oliver Bude: Dudley Sutton
Kenneth Lowrie: Bob Peck
Dennis Mulley: Bernard Lloyd
Andy Anderson: Trevor Peacock
Austin Purvis: Hugh Paddick
J.J. Farr: Albert Finney

Director: Ronald Eyre
Lighting: Rick Fisher

Timon of Athens
by William Shakespeare
16 February 1988
The Studio, Haymarket Theatre,
Leicester.

Poet/
Sempronius: Andrew Johnson
Painter/
Timandra: Sharon Stephens
Timon: Guy Williams
Lucius/
1st Senator: Martin Bax
Apemantus: Anthony Douse
Alcibaides: Brian Bovell
Flavius: Philip Brook

Director: Simon Usher
Assistant Director: David O'Shea
Music: Gavin Bryars
Lighting: Sam Garwood

The Trackers of Oxyrhynchus
by Tony Harrison
12 July 1988
Ancient Stadium of Delphi, Greece.

Grenfell/Apollo: Jack Shepherd
Hunt/Silenus: Barrie Rutter
Kyllene: Juliet Stevenson
Hermes: Dave Hill
Chorus of Fellaheens/Satrys/
Football hooligans:
Peter Andrew
Christopher Beck
Lawrence Evans
Billy Fellows
Dave Hill
John O'Hara
Philip Middlemiss
Stephen Petcher
Simon Rackham
Clive Rowe

Director: Tony Harrison
Composer: Stephen Edwards
Assistant to
the Designer: Vicki Hallam

Julius Caesar
by William Shakespeare
9 September 1988
Leicester Haymarket Theatre.

Julius Caesar: Robert Flemyng
Octavius
Caesar: Delaval Astley
Marcus Antony: Martin McKellan
Lepidus: Richard Willams
Cicero: Delaval Astley
Publius: Richard Williams
Popilius Lena: Peter Lovstrom
Brutus: Joseph Marcell

Cassius: Stephen Boxer
Casca: William Key
Trebonius: Duncan Law
Ligarius: Richard Williams
Decius Brutus: Robert Blythe
Metellus
Cimber: Gil Sutherland
Cinna: Philip Brook
Flavius: Gil Sutherland
Marullus: Duncan Law
Artemidorus: Gil Sutherland
A Soothsayer: Richard Williams
Cinna the poet: Duncan Law
Messala: Robert Blythe
Titinius: Philip Brook
Pindarus: Duncan Law
Lucius: Milind Arolker
Lucius: Sandip Mistry
Calphurnia: Jacqueline
Dankworth
Portia: Janet Key
Servant: Cathy Finlay
Tamsin Olivier

Director: John Dexter
Lighting
Designer: Andy Phillips
Music: Stephen Boxer

Creon
by Stephen Spender

Oedipus at
Thebes: Stephen Boxer
Oedipus at
Colonus: Robert Flemyng
Creon: Joseph Marcell
Polyneices: Martin McKellan
Tiresias: Richard Williams
Haemon: Peter Lovstrom
Theseus: Robert Blythe
Gardener: Philip Brook
First Soldier: Gil Sutherland
Second Soldier: Duncan Law
Messenger: Delaval Astley
Antigone: Tamsin Olivier
Ismene: Cathy Finlay
Chorus: Stephen Boxer
Jacqueline Dankworth
Janet Key
William Key

Director: John Dexter
Lighting
Designer: Andy Phillips
Music: Stephen Boxer

The March on Russia
by David Storey
6 April 1989
The National Theatre in the
Lyttelton.

Colin: Frank Grimes
Pasmore: Bill Owen
Mrs Pasmore: Constance Chapman
Wendy: Rosemary Martin
Eileen: Patsy Rowlands
Postman: Michael Goldie

Director: Lindsay Anderson
Lighting: Mick Hughes
Music: Alan Price
Design
Assistant: Kate Robertson

The Threepenny Opera
by Bertolt Brecht
4 November 1989
Lunt-Fontanne Theatre, New York.

A Ballad Singer: Ethyl Eichelberger
Jenny Diver: Suzanne Douglas

Jonathan
Jeremiah
Peachum: Alvin Epstein
Filch: Jeff Blumenkrantz
Mrs Peachum: Georgia Brown
Polly Peachum: Maureen McGovern
Macheath: Sting
Matt of the
Mint: Josh Mostel
Crook-Finger
Jack: Mitchell Greenberg
Sawtooth Bob: David Schechter
Ed: Philip Carroll
Walter: Tom Robbins
Jimmy: Alex Santoriello
Tiger Brown: Larry Marshall
Dolly: Anne Kerry Ford
Betty: Jan Horvath
Vixen: Teresa de Zarn
Molly: Nancy Ringham
Suky Tawdry: K.T. Sullivan
Old Whore: Fiddle Viracola
Smith: David Pursley
Policemen: MacIntyre Dixon
Michael Piontek
Lucy: Kim Criswell
Beggars,
Bystanders: Philip Carroll
MacIntyre Dixon
Michael Piontek
David Schechter
Steven Major West

Director: John Dexter
Misic Director: Julius Rudel
Lighting: Andy Phillips &
Brian Nason

Square Rounds
by Tony Harrison
1 October 1992
The Royal National Theatre in the
Olivier.

Munitionette/
Sir William
Crookes: Gillian Barge
Munitionette: Jo Cameron Brown
Munitionette: Helen Chadwick
Mary Chater
Munitionette/
Hiram Maxim: Paola Dionisotti
Munitionette/
Clara Haber: Maria Friedman
Munitionette/
Hudson
Maxim: Jenny Galloway
Munitionette: Elaine Hallam
Sue Holland
Munitionette/
Fritz Haber: Sara Kestelman
Munitionette: Sonya Leite
Maggie McCarthy
Myra McFadyen
Jane Nash
Theresa Petts
Juliet Prague
Emma Rogers
Mandy Short
Munitionette/
Justus von
Liebig: Sian Thomas
Munitionette/
Lady Nellie
Crookes: Angela Tunstall
Munitionette: Catherine White
Shell-Shocked
Man & Chinese
Magician: Arturo Bracchetti
Sweeper
Mawes: Harry Towb

Director: Tony Harrison
Lighting: Mick Hughes
Music: Dominic
Muldowney

Choreographer: Lawrence Evans
Magic
Consultant: Ali Bongo

Assistant to Designer Polly Richards

Stages
by David Storey
18 November 1992
The Royal National Theatre in the
Cottesloe.

Karen: Gabrielle Lloyd
Fenchurch: Alan Bates
Bea: Marjorie Yates
Marion: Joanna David
Rebecca: Rosemary Martin
Director: Lindsay Anderson
Lighting: Mick Hughes
Music: Alan Price

Index